Adventuring in Adoption

By LEE M. BROOKS

and EVELYN C. BROOKS

Adventuring

in

Adoption

CHAPEL HILL

THE UNIVERSITY OF NORTH CAROLINA PRESS

For Robert

Foreword

BY ERNEST R. GROVES

This book has been greatly needed. In spite of the wide-spread and increasing interest in adoption of children, information of value to adoptive parents and social workers has been scattered and for many of the former unavailable. Now we have not only a much desired book but one that is built upon serious interest, personal experience, and accurate and discerning scholarship.

The authors, realizing how useful the right kind of book on adoption would be, went at their task with the thoroughness of well-trained students and with an understanding that has come in part from their personal experience as adoptive parents and in part from their investigation of the problems of adoption from the point of view both of families and of institutions. They have given us a book that bears evidence of its unhurried preparation and practical motive. It is clear, usable, and authoritative. Popular in form, it is soundly scientific, advancing from matters that concern the parents of the child to theoretic and fundamental problems of concern to the serious student of adoption. Although primarily written for adoptive parents, social workers and other professions dealing with children will find it indispensable.

There is every reason for supposing that the adoption of children will become in our American life of greater and greater importance. There seems to be good evidence that the strain of our difficult, complicated, and in great measure discordant, modern life will, in the case of persons organically highly sensitive, adversely affect fertility. The popularizing of birth control will lead often, with the best of motives, many young people to avoid children during the time when, if ever, they are fertile. As a consequence of these two influences, the number of high-class, conscientious families seeking to adopt children will certainly not grow smaller. On the other hand, our placing societies are sure to lift their standards and to insist upon greater adequacy and responsibility in the families to which they allow their children to go on probation. This means that useful as this book by Dr. Lee M. Brooks and Evelyn C. Brooks, his wife, is at present, in the days near at hand it will be even more needed.

Chapel Hill, North Carolina
February 1, 1939

Introduction

Originality is exceeding rare. The more one writes the more conscious one becomes of indebtedness to others and perhaps this is doubled when two essay to work together. In our aim to produce a helpful book on adoption we have attempted to bring through the unity of our own thinking over the years, an understandable patterning of the diverse threads of much that has been said and written on the subject. Into the whole we have woven our own experience as adoptive parents.

From adoptive homes, parents and children, and from research by others we have gained much primary and secondary material for which we are, of course, greatly indebted. We have deliberately freed our pages of footnotes because of the nature and purpose of the book, preferring to point the way to sources, for students and others interested in further reading, through the annotated bibliography.

The first seven chapters (Part I) are primarily for adoptive families and all others who, in prospect or in retrospect, are interested in a nontechnical discussion of the subject. The last seven chapters (Part II) are aimed at the interests of those who see the adopted child as a focus of parental and professional responsibility and who wish to explore the broader field of adoption.

To many libraries, with a special salute to the University of North Carolina staff and facilities, we give our thanks. The assistance proffered and given in time and talent by the University of North Carolina Law School, especially by Miss Lucille Elliott, has been immeasurably helpful.

For criticism, contribution, and encouragement we are grateful to experienced social workers, lawyers, executives, and colleagues among whom are Benjamin R. Andrews, Margaret G. Bourne, C. C. Carstens, Albert Coates, Ernest H. Cole, Ernest R. Groves, Shelby M. Harrison, Katharine P. Hewins, Katharine Jocher, George H. Lawrence, Howard W. Odum, Sarah H. Spencer, and James M. Verner. Among those students whose thoughts and graduate theses have worked along with ours are Gertrude B. Jones, Jacqueline Johnson Simpson, and Frederick B. Parker. While grateful for the assistance that has come so generously, especially for the responsiveness of the Child Welfare League of America and the Children's Bureau, we alone stand responsible for the content of our book, its emphasis, philosophy, and interpretations.

Finally, deepest gratitude to our son, long since merged in the flow of our family life, and now a schoolboy in the widening stream of community experience—to him, how much we owe!

L. M. B.

Chapel Hill, North Carolina
January, 1939

E. C. B.

Contents

PART I

PRIMARILY FOR ADOPTIVE FAMILIES
AND ALL OTHERS WHO, IN PROS-
PECT OR IN RETROSPECT, ARE IN-
TERESTED IN A NONTECHNICAL
DISCUSSION OF ADOPTION

The Adopter Speaks

"Adoption is a great adventure, comparable only to the thrill of actual, physiological motherhood, and in some ways surpassing even that. Having tried both, I can state from experience that the child you deliberately choose rewards your love and care just as richly as the one Mother Nature sends haphazard." This conviction voiced by a mother amid the gloom of depression and war-threatened years, is but a reflection of what many others have said with enthusiasm.

For many reasons—economic, social, and political—the adoption of children is today a subject of rapidly growing interest in the civilized world. Its place in folkway and law is being scrutinized in nations of every continent. The United States Children's Bureau, the Child Welfare League of America, and the League of Nations are among the major contributors in a continuing program of study and legislative reform. Academic research proceeds with vigor; the press abounds with human interest material.

Various aspects of adoption have been dealt with over and over in recent years in all sorts of magazines and newspapers. In this book we aim to touch helpfully some of the major problems; we are not attempting to answer "all your doubts and questions about adoption" as was the expressed intent of a short article a few years ago.

Since our emphasis is upon the young child, we do not deal with adoption of older children and adults. We have tried to be fairly precise in our use of the word "adoption" which implies permanence of legal custody and full family membership. The foster relationship is generally less binding and less permanent though "foster" is often used in references to adoption. Only when the final decree is granted does the child of other parents become the same as one's own child.

While some of the writing on adoption has inclined to the sentimental more than to the mental, there have been numerous valuable and substantial contributions, especially from parents themselves. Reliable testimony also comes from the files of child welfare workers, doctors, judges, and students of the family, all the more impressive because not intended for publication. Here the adoptive parents, and in some cases the adopted children as well, write thoughtfully and deliberately, not for effect but in a straightforward attempt to describe their experience.

What do some of them have to say?

A frail mother, deterred from a second adoption only by lack of physical strength, insists that "blood is strong but love is stronger."

A physician and his wife into whose hands fell a weak mite of babyhood, speak of their beloved *daughter:* "For humanity's sake we took the little thing weighing only two and one-half pounds. She had to have the greatest care to live at all. We had little time to think it over; something had to be done at once; we did it and we are glad." Here the sequence seemed to be responsibility, responsiveness, and inseparability.

One adoptive mother looked for seven years before she found just the right baby, "a foundling of eight months, an adorable child, and now a charming woman of twenty-six, mother of one of the most desirable sons you could find. I can assure you no prouder grandparents live than my husband and myself, yet we are *just* foster parents."

Still another mother whose five own children were nearly grown, took a baby to board temporarily and finally adopted her. To a friend she confides: "Not one of my own children has been as thoughtful or lovely as Elizabeth. She has brought sunshine and happiness." Elizabeth herself, when asked where she would most like to be, replied: "Right where I am with my wonderful family."

For those who would magnify the hazards involved, a specialist in child welfare suggests that the adoption of children is no more risky than most of life's adventures. As one adoptive mother puts it: "You ordinarily know far less about the eugenic history of your husband's family than you do about the ancestry of the child you have adopted under proper conditions." We deal with this further in the chapter on "Facts or Fears."

Somewhat vehemently affirms this adoptive parent: "Right here I should like to meet and slay the great giant bugaboo that deters most childless couples (those who genuinely fear, not those who rationalize) from venturing forth on the quest—that bugaboo question, 'How do you know the child will turn out well?' I answer by putting another query: 'How do we know we are going to turn out well as parents?'" Other adoptive parents, among the many who have shared their experiences so generously with us, have similarly pointed out that whenever a child is adopted, parents are adopted too.

A question that troubles a considerable number of people is this: How can we know that the child selected will be the best one *for us?* As in all human plans, certainty is elusive here also. Surely there is a large element of chance in all germ plasm inheritance. No parent can order the qualities of his offspring in advance. The question, however valid it is, should not be overweighed. After a child has been pronounced physically sound and mentally promising —this implying a reasonable check on heredity where pos-

sible—there is little to fear. There is every reason to believe that the relationship will deepen and grow toward complete satisfaction. Growth, adaptation, and affection have a
way of blending. "He becomes your own inseparably," as
one adopter has expressed it, "as dear as any child of the
flesh. No matter what he is like, it seems to be the only way
you would have it after he has been with you a while."

Adoption is a social type of birth the moment the final
decree is granted. Bound by legal ties after adequate examinations and investigations have been made, the adopted
child's position in the family is rightly as irrevocable as
though he had been decreed through biological birth for
that particular family.

To a large extent the desire for children, whether through
biological or adoptive parenthood, is the same. Perhaps
such differences as exist are of degree or of emphasis rather
than of kind. The person of strong family attachment who
anticipates pleasure in tracing likenesses to his kinfolk or
his mate, may perhaps hesitate to accept the substitute of
adoption. Yet even those, in whom this clan feeling seems
to be uppermost, often find satisfaction in centering on the
growth of fine family qualities such as loyalty, honesty, and
dependability, and are perchance surprised, as are many parents, to find that their children are growing to resemble them
in physical characteristics as well.

Foremost among the motives that impel toward the rear-
ing of children is the need for response. It may be recognized only in the vaguest terms, as a "hunger of the heart";
or it may be faced as a desire too elemental to deny, whatever the cost. The impulse does not occur with equal po-
tency in all individuals, but, granting this, it is not safe to
assume that it is lacking because at present unfelt or un-
recognized. This need for response may merely be un-
awakened, depending as it does upon emotional maturity,
degree of absorption in business or profession, number and

closeness of social contacts, and various other factors. Nor can outward expression be considered a measure of this inner and spiritual demand. The gushing person who indulges in baby-talk and lavishes caresses and unsuitable toys is exhibiting less capacity for true parenthood than the more controlled person who thinks and acts in terms of the child's needs.

Many people now believe that what has been uncritically termed "maternal instinct," a mysterious complex of knowledge and devotion that blossoms suddenly at the physical birth of a child, is nothing more or less than the acceptance of parental responsibility, something *learned,* and then fixed by habit.

The socially mature person, man or woman, is touched by helplessness, particularly in a child. If that child has a claim upon him, he rises to the occasion whether the immediate need is physical or economic or spiritual. That there is any hard and fast division of labor or proportioning of affection is an absurdity.

A word may here be said in behalf of fathers. While both popular and scientific writing has had much to say in the last decade about marriage as a full partnership, it is still too often assumed that the male parent functions mainly on a biologic and economic level. Men, on the whole, are keenly alert to childhood's needs. Certainly a man is as quick to snatch a child from physical danger as a woman. Often a father proves to be a tireless nurse and many a bereft home finds the father doing the mothering extremely well.

It may be true that more women than men "make a fuss" over children but it would be interesting to know how much genuine feeling such superficial expressions indicate. May they not be a carry-over from the time, not so far distant, when all women were expected to make kitchen and children their sole interest? Old folkways and old folk-thoughts are very tenacious. In these days of small families many a man, and woman too, has grown up deprived of intimacies with little children. Small wonder if such a person is indifferent or overattentive to such children as he encounters. Wise ways of dealing with little folks have to be learned like any other social art. Whoever feels that an own mother is closer than the father to the child by reason of physical bond must admit that adoptive parents start on an equal footing.

By their own testimony, in some adoptive homes the desire for a child first stirs in the father; in others the mother takes the initiative; and in many households it is a coequal adventure from the start, probably in much the same distribution as in birth-giving families, if the truth were known. Some of the mothers who admit they had to win over their husbands in the first place, say that after the child became a member of the family there was no difference in parental feeling. Several proclaim that the fathers have come to have a more devoted and demonstrative affection. One man, so austere that his own sons stood in awe of him, showed only the greatest tenderness for his frail adopted daughter.

An eager adoptive father insisted that his wife should go off for a day and leave their six-months-old baby in his care, so desirous was he of getting acquainted with the little stranger. When she hesitated on the grounds that he would not know how to give a bath and sterilize bottles, he reminded her that he knew as much as she had known when she undertook the task a few days before. It was this same father who found a way, two or three years later, to tell the little fellow of his adoption, and who taught the first lessons in sportsmanship on the golf course and the football field. Parenthood was life's great adventure for him, and friends were surprised to glimpse the poet that had been hiding within the business executive. Yet his sense of reality was never submerged, for upon his untimely death a few years later it was disclosed that he had arranged a life insurance policy for his son's education on the first anniversary of the baby's adoption.

A woman who had been adopted in infancy writes this at the age of thirty-seven: "Mother would have liked a large family but father was opposed to this and had to be prevailed upon considerably to have me. However, let me say that he was and is the dearest parent a child could possibly have. I have heard relatives say that before he had me, father paid little or no attention to their own children and there was considerable surprise that he was so completely wrapped up in me. . . . There have been times when I felt closer to my father than to mother and usually this has been when I was in some difficulty. I could calmly talk it over with him but mother was inclined to be extremely nervous. As I look back I think many times that both parents overindulged me. They both worked and sacrificed so that I might have the advantages of a college education. Certainly I received as much affection and perhaps more than most own children."

Who would not agree that affection has an important, even indispensable part, in the emotional development of members of a family? It may be, with so many functions of the family being transferred to outside agencies—religious training, education, housekeeping details—that the mutual tenderness and attachment growing out of close association and common interest are the greatest contribution of the present-day home. Outside contacts are increasingly formal or casual, outside activities, more and more strenuous and crowded. At home we need the warmth of understanding, the assurance of steady devotion, the stimulation of undemanding affection, that a well-knit family circle can supply. The evidence is strong that the adoptive home does not lag behind the natural one in the production of these qualities.

Of a twenty-year-old son, adopted in infancy, a father writes in a letter: "You know how we are about Jerry. We are still as silly about him as when he was a baby and he is about us. . . . We love him and are satisfied with him." The life history of another family is glimpsed in these few lines: "We are very proud of our little adopted daughter and love her as dearly as our own son, nineteen months younger. Our first baby died at birth and it seemed as if Doris was my own brought back to me. There could be no greater love than we have for her and she has certainly returned it."

Another example of the interplay of family affection comes from a mother of an own and an adopted child: "Upon my word of honor if I had to decide between my own boy and my adopted daughter I could only say, 'Thy will be done!' Her father feels the same way. Our girl is gifted in music and our son gave up his chance so that she might study. He knows that she is adopted but says she is the sweetest sister in the world."

Such affirmations might be multiplied many times but none could be found of greater interest than this picture of a developing family relationship, as told by the adoptive mother: "One day when Ruth was in second grade I heard a commotion in the hall below. I looked over the banister and there was Ruth with a troop of strange children. I thought she looked rather defiant though she was being unusually polite. From room to room they went. I heard her saying such things as this, 'my father's picture'; 'that belongs to my big brother in college'; 'this is sister and her hair is curly and very pretty.' On they went and a door swung open. 'My room, my baby doll that Santa Claus brought me, my books and I can take them to school if I want to.' Then straight to my room they came. 'This is my mamma. May I give them some cake, mamma?' I knew the zero hour had come and I determined to bear her up even if supper was a little short. 'Surely you may. It is yours and you may do as you like.' When they were gone I asked, 'Who were your friends?' 'Oh, they were just children; they kept saying, " 'Tain't *your* house, 'tain't *your* mamma," and lots of things like that till I was tired, so I invited them home to see.' "

Here then is a cross-section of "honest" opinion, not academic, not theoretical, not journalistic. We have gathered it, mostly at first hand, to put into words a bit of actual adoptive experience and to pass on to other interested persons whatever of value it may have. Here, adoptive parents and adopted children as well, just average folks like most of us, have described and analyzed their feelings and attitudes.

If these expressions and others to be found on succeeding pages serve as helps to people traveling along the same road, the main purpose of the book will be served. If, in addition, a few students and others reach a more comprehensive and unbiased view of adoption, find it a promising field for further exploration, an inviting avenue of vocational choice; or if a specialist in one of the professions concerned with adoption is enabled to see it in better proportion, then the goal of our efforts will have been achieved.

2

Facts or Fears

Too many people worry overmuch about the lineage of the child, whether their own or one considered for adoption. Unwise, of course, would be anyone who discounted the great importance of reasonable inquiry into heredity, but the tendency has been to stress heredity and to discount environment. In this connection more facts will mean fewer fears.

One of the scientific blessings of this century is a better understanding of nature and nurture, the reciprocal relationship between seed and soil. We know today that the power within the seed awaits the power of soil and climate and the skill of the cultivator. We are surer than ever that the civilized environment calls forth qualities and capacities that are similar, if not identical, throughout mankind. Science has been uncovering facts that mean for the family, and particularly for the adoptive parent and child, a welcome emancipation from fear. There is comfort in the belief of modern biology that, as Dr. H. S. Jennings puts it, "whatever the environment brings out is hereditary."

Yet facts get tangled, if not strangled, by tyrannical words and slogans. "Heredity," used with finality, has led to misunderstanding. "Environment" also is in danger of becoming a worn-out coin that slips through uninformed slot-machine discussion into erroneous dogmatism. It really was news when, as a challenge to complacent belief in sayings, somebody went to the trouble of making a silk purse out of a sow's ear.

Mother Nature does not worry at all about our labels or interpretations but she must smile when someone confidently asserts that heredity is three, or even seven times as powerful as environment. In thousands of ways over thousands of years she has patiently been revealing that good soil (environment) plus good seed (heredity) produce good results (adjusted living things); that in the imperishable chemistry of earthly materials the cultivation of either soil or seed or both can transform the poor into the fair, the fair into the good, the good into the excellent.

Nor is environment the exceedingly slow moving influence it was once thought to be. Many children born in America of immigrant parents have been compared with their fellows born abroad in the parent countries, and it has been discovered that the American born children show changes in stature, hair, and skin. Even head form seems to yield slightly to the new environment. The earlier theory of anthropologist Franz Boas seems to have confirmation in the more recent findings of H. L. Shapiro; for example, Hawaiian-born Japanese "far exceed their contemporaries in Japan" in height.

"Heredity" is still used as a blanket to cover a host of conditions which *appear* to be hereditary but which are in no sense explainable by germ cell life and chemistry. Many a little adoptee walks, talks, gesticulates, and even looks like one or the other of the adopting parents! Diseases are no more *established* in the germ cells than is an automobile accident. Nor is there yet any reliable evidence that the ambitious mother can shape the artistic destiny of her child by thought and action in those prenatal (environmental) days as she waits hopefully for the birth. Another very common mistake is to confuse the congenital with the hereditary. Syphilis, impossible to inherit through the germ cell,

may be contracted congenitally, which is really environmental contamination. Also, calcium in the expectant
mother's food has much to do with the child's lifelong tooth
structure while iodine deficiency may contribute to defective
offspring. Such illustrations of congenital influence point
directly at environment and not at heredity, for heredity's
work was finished the moment conception took place in the
fusion of male and female germ cells.

Heredity, scientifically considered, is like a very complex
card game with many symbols and innumerable possible
combinations. The germ cells contain arrangements of
chemicals which interact in an orderly way in the process
of development, but these germ-chemicals are always conditioned by the environment. It cannot be emphasized too
often, in view of former opinion, that the characteristics of
the adult are not inflexibly established in miniature in the
germ cells. Proper materials are essential, of course, but
these materials or chemicals of heredity must interact fit-
tingly with each other and with their environment. Experiments with fruit flies, salamanders, and other organisms
clearly substantiate this point. Often we have presented
to us the picture of the degenerate family and its tragic
progeny. Seldom in the delineation of such infamous families is there emphasis upon the soil or environmental factors.
In short, heredity cannot be discussed as a phenomenon by
itself because not only seed but also soil and other conditions
determine what the fruitage will be.

In the long stream of heredity the immediate parents are
a by-pool with preceding generations making immeasurable
contributions, and for this reason it is possible to give too
much credit or debit to the child's father and mother. It
must not be forgotten that multiple mixing has resulted
in the flow through four grandparents, eight great-
grandparents, sixteen great-great-grandparents, and so on.
Nature is the great protector, averager, and distributor of

functions and abilities. People unfamiliar with Nature's care of germ continuity occasionally have fears concerning the parental soundness of individuals maimed in accidents and war. Recently there appeared a news item about the Yugoslav village of Vetrenik where a few years ago the government gave to each of thirty blind veterans a cottage and equipment for light farming. Wives were then procured for each man by advertisement. More than one hundred children have been born without a single case of blindness. The long-standing provision for sight in the germ cell, thousands of generations of it for each soldier, could not be disturbed by acquired blindness that bore no relation to the hereditary condition of eyes. We are, then, but part of a stream into which countless currents have poured for ages past.

That Nature is resourceful and kindly in her ways is apparent on every hand. She works endlessly to effect better and better adjustments, especially with lower animals who do not interfere with her processes. Protective coloring on the rabbit, a warmer coat on wind-swept cattle, a little fuzz on fruit flies experimentally bred in the refrigerator—about all these organic changes she seems to say: "I'll help you by stimulating into activity those chemical properties within you that will adjust you to these particular conditions." Is there not a suggestion here that mental and social adaptations can be called forth as well as organic adjustment? In her ample bosom there overflows a stream of life that makes no social distinctions. She sends forth the ingredients of the genius and the imbecile with little discrimination between poverty area and boulevard.

It is man himself who is responsible not only for ideas of blood lineage tinged with snobbery but also for the conditions that have meant the building of barriers and special privileges. This by no means affirms that all men are created equal nor does it imply that eugenic effort for race improvement is not highly desirable. It does mean, however, that lowly parentage will continue to produce genius and that "first families" cannot be insured against nitwits. We have seen an Abraham Lincoln, a Booker Washington, a Michael Pupin, a Toyohiko Kagawa, and others emerge from obscure corners of poverty and disadvantage. What else than the environment brought out their qualities of leadership? Contemplate the pre-Christian occupants of the British Isles; undersized, hairy savages, ancestors to many of us. Do we pause before we boast of our pure Anglo-Saxon blood? (Another worn-out word-coin for the museum!) We of Nordic pride would do well to give more attention to the environmental rock from which we were hewn.

What the union of any two adults will produce cannot be predicted. Every ovum and every spermatazoön have different possibilities. One ovum and one spermatazoön unite; conception has taken place; in due time a child is born. From these same two parents what chance is there that any other two cells thus uniting would have produced the *same* baby? The likelihood is so slight, one in so many millions of billions, that we are staggered even as in contemplating stellar space. Up to the birth of the child, the role of parents is mechanical, but once birth has taken place, the demands are far greater than can be met by any automatic functioning. The peculiarly *human* part of the child's life begins *after* he is born.

Thus we come to a conclusion especially pertinent to adoption, namely that *efficient parenthood is primarily sociological rather than biological.* What is done with a child after he is born counts more than the circumstances of his birth. He holds possibilities within himself which parental influence and general environment can either develop or crush. To Nature must be added Nurture.

People often come to agencies torn between the desire to adopt and the fear of doing so. How will the child turn out? Isn't he in danger of inheriting bad traits from his parents and coming to a bad end in spite of all we can do? Probably no greater risk is taken in adopting a child than in propagating one's own. A family with a clean heredity for generations may, without warning, produce a defective or a ne'er-do-well who happens to have shuffled into his make-up a deal of the undesirable qualities of his ancestors.

Does an expectant mother, however eugenic her interests and background may be, *know* that her child will be normal? She can only hope. On the other hand, the normality of a three-months-old baby waiting for adoption can be ascertained up to a certain point at least. Just what his I. Q. will be cannot be determined, of course. But the agency candidate for adoption has escaped the grosser feeblemindedness that so often comes from childbirth injuries, since a child several months old would already have revealed the crudities of such an existing deficiency.

In brief, a prospective foster home has little to fear in selecting a child a few months old through an approved placement agency where reasonable inquiry into the heredity has been made with satisfactory results. Consider the interesting fact that the foster parent does not appear on the scene until someone else has run the early, major hazards of childbearing! He can choose, he does not have to take what comes along.

"The only thing I ask of the baby," says one happy adoptive parent, "is a sound, healthy body. I'll take care of the rest. I'm going to adopt another child within a year. As for our Anne, she was one of six left stranded by a deserted mother. She was a strong-willed little thing and no one seemed to want her. The other five children had all been adopted. Today at the age of ten, Anne is still determined and strong-minded, but sweet tempered, easily managed, and most trustworthy." The immediate heredity of this child was somewhat questionable. The adoptive

parents state that their interest in her background is concerned only with "guarding against pitfalls and encouraging
tendencies that look good. She is very much pleased when
someone mentions that she looks like her mother. Indeed
she is almost gleeful when some unknowing person makes
such a comment, for doesn't she know that she is not our
flesh and blood! Let me add this also: she has many of
our mannerisms and characteristics. This fact interests me
greatly because I, as well as my friends, had in so many
instances looked upon child-parent similarities of speech and
body movement as inherited when doubtless so many of
them are merely copied by the child. Well, we are very
proud of Anne, proud to hear her call us mother and father,
proud to know that she is *our* child."

The older child may also find a haven. Into a physician's
family, already possessed of four own children, came a little
eleven-year-old orphan girl. "She was of a poor family none
of whose members had amounted to much. Her care had
been such as a stone-blind mother could render. The child
was crude, 'a hopeless case,' at least so some people thought.
Anyway she became our child. We treated her as if she
had been our very own. She grew up to be a very fine
woman and at this time holds a responsible position in the
government of a large city. To say that we are thankful
and that she is also, is to put it mildly."

Like the gardener who hopefully cultivates thrifty seed-
lings that others have planted, this mother says of the little
brother and sister adopted five years ago: "No matter
where we take them we hear no end of praise in such words
as 'how well-mannered,' 'such lovely children.' We never
were very successful in ascertaining much about their background, other than that they were abandoned by their own
mother when they were very small."

Not without a smile can we observe the enthusiasm of
those who know full well that parental love for children is

nourished by contact rather than something started and maintained by instinct. Asks one mother: "Why so much raving about one's 'own' child! What pitiful, yet lovable but unloved children have we all seen beneath the roof and domination of 'own' parents; neglect and ignorance instead of the intelligent care and the strong fabric of understanding that we think of as home. I have two adopted girls. One came to us at eight months, an adorable foundling child. Now she is a charming woman of twenty-six, herself the mother of a splendid son. True, she married a fine man. She knows about her past and has absorbed it all without any personality scars. My other girl I took when she was six, a frail child, now strong and doing well in high school." Thus does this mother, a nurse, feel vigorously about the power of environment.

All the foregoing sketches depict successes in adoption. Are there no failures? Indeed there are, and it may be added that not all "own" children measure up to parental hopes, for alas, there is nothing in heredity that guarantees any family against prodigal sons and wayward daughters.

Much has been said about illegitimacy and bad blood; more has been thought furtively than has been said; too much has been whispered. "Oh, didn't you know that the child's mother was never married? I've heard . . ." (buzz-z-z hums the busy little bee of gossip). The objectively minded person asks this question: Why should the average illegitimate child be less promising than the average legitimate offspring of the thoughtless and unplanned or the love-at-first-sight sort of ceremonialized union? Germ cells and their chemicals know no ritual; they neither hear nor heed it; they know only the law of life and so far as biology is concerned, they know only legitimacy. Parents may be illegitimate, but both science and religion proclaim it false so to label a blameless child. As for inferior or bad blood, enough is known about dominant and recessive character-

istics to indicate the dangers implied in the term. Neither
marriage nor adoption should ignore the meaning of hereditary taints appearing in the family line, especially where such
defects are suspected of existing on both sides of the families
concerned. Here the red light may well be flashed. Even
so we cannot see further than the first bend in the river.
The fact is that adoption has become a common and approved solution for the nurture of illegitimate, or what some
have termed prenuptial or "natural" children.

Court statistics indicate that at least sixty per cent of
the adoption petitions granted are for so-called illegitimate
children. A few years ago we made the following inquiry
of sixty adoptive families: "Will people who really want
to adopt a child consider illegitimacy a barrier?" Fifty-five
answered, "No"; one thought it might be an obstacle; two
were in doubt; and two did not respond. By no means were
all the children in these homes "illegitimate." At any rate
a goodly number of eugenists believe the ancestry of such
children is likely to be better than that of "legitimate"
children dumped on the market for adoption.

"Am I willing to accept a child born out of wedlock?"
The answer hinges on feelings and prejudices. If a stigma
seems to attach to such a child, full and free parent-child
interchange may be jeopardized. Great love is possible
only between equals. Nothing could be more fatal to the
growth of affection than for one to feel superior while the
other knows himself to be looked down upon, whether or
not there is any real basis of inequality. The small child
seems almost clairvoyant in making his judgments of people.
However much his elders seek to hide their true feelings,
he sees through their dissemblings though he may not at
the moment be able to interpret them. And whatever cloak
of polite pretense we habitually wear, the daily association
of family life will at times tear it from our shoulders.

More than one behavior problem has arisen from a hidden

antagonism that made a child feel discriminated against so that he became a bully or too humble and overanxious to please. Nor has the relationship a wholesome foundation if the foster parents feel too sorry for their child, for they will be in danger of spoiling him in their effort to over-compensate, to make up to him for what they feel he has missed. This may be especially true when he has been adopted by relatives.

The best home is the one where the child is loved and accepted by emotionally well-poised adults, where he is respected simply and naturally for himself alone without reference to his antecedents. If for any reason his earlier experience is such that it smolders in memory, a blast of parental emotion may fan a flame that consumes or scars the parent-child relationship. Even in an ordinarily controlled and considerate family the child is occasionally hurt spiritually. A behavior crisis may provoke such a shocking remark as: "Nothing better could be expected of such a lowborn person as you." Perhaps a surprise; certainly a jolt! So much more dangerous and damaging for the personality of a foster child than for an own child. For that matter, who has not heard one parent of an own child speak bitingly of the mate's blood ancestry: "That kid gets his mean traits from your tribe, not mine!" (If you have escaped such homes ablaze, social workers have not.) Emotional and social maturity is not necessarily parallel with chronological age. Some people never grow up emotionally.

As for the actual risks in adopting the "illegitimate" child, they are probably on the whole considerably less than for the other types available for adoption. This is especially true if he is taken in infancy before he has a chance to be mishandled and if it can be ascertained that he is free from the grosser hereditary or congenital taints. If the heritage is known to be good there can be little to fear. Many reputable agencies now keep children whose ancestry is not verifiable under scrutiny for several months, during which period frequent physical and mental tests are made as a safeguard for careful adopters.

Many of the adoptable "legitimate" children are those abandoned by their parents or taken from them by the court because of unfit home conditions such as feeblemindedness, drunkenness, disorderliness, failure to support a decent standard of living, low morals, and the like. It may be expected that these children will have a poor inheritance. It is certain that their care and training have been inadequate. Yet miracles have been wrought: misshapen infants, pop-eyed from hunger and illness, pitiful to behold, have been restored to attractive childhood by proper care. While many children seem unsuitable for anything but institutional or boarding foster home care, there are those who promise well, such as orphans whose parents had made no provision for them. These are set forth as candidates for adoption. The institution, however, is the happiest solution for the greatly handicapped who in most normal situations will find themselves seriously, if not hopelessly inferior.

Granted that the adopters are willing to accept an illegitimate child, what are the chief points to consider? First, find out as much as possible about his background so as to treat wisely his asset and liability tendencies. Those assets or good qualities in his grandparental and parental past, if known, can be worked upon, can be encouraged later; the liability or undesirable points can be discouraged. Also, when he is old enough to understand, the important facts of his birth will almost inevitably be called for. Memory is treacherous and life none too certain. It is a safeguard to put in writing briefly all the pertinent material, to be placed with the family documents such as wills and life insurance policies against the time of need. Adopted children too often reach adulthood without being able to find out enough about their ancestral traits to know whether they have a right to impose them upon posterity. If the biological heritage is good, it will give the child confidence; if it is not good he should have a chance to face it gradually and constructively while his foster parents are at hand to give him guidance and courage. The shock of knowing about the hidden past suddenly in a crisis, as on the eve of marriage or of a business venture, may prove disastrous; still more disastrous never to find it out until he becomes the father of a defective child or goes to pieces under a strain to which his narrow margin of nervous reserve should not have been subjected.

When it is said that the child born out of wedlock is a reasonably good risk, it is said with some reservations. Few prostitutes have children because they practice contraception and because their business often renders them sterile. Such offspring as they have are unsafe because of the danger of congenital venereal disease. Their babies are not offered for adoption by careful placing agencies. The girl from a home of low standards is more likely to keep her child because very often her group attaches less stigma to births out of wedlock. This is particularly true of marginal, simpler peoples. But the high school or college girl, so sheltered that she does not know how to protect herself when she chooses to make a social misstep, often finds her family irrevocably opposed to recognizing her child. Life is unimaginable without the financial and social support to which she is accustomed, and she is so emotionally immature that the infant has little or no interest for her. Or it may be, if she is away from home, she keeps the whole affair a secret from her parents. If her partner is a schoolmate or other young friend, experimental rather than vicious, her child is likely to be biologically acceptable. In such cases the placing agency can give assurance of hereditary soundness that may safely be relied upon, even though confidential details may be withheld which, under our present social customs, might be embarrassing if not damaging to the persons concerned.

In conclusion, biology tells us that what the environment brings out must have existed in the individual or it would not have appeared. Heredity is very largely a phenomenon of chemistry, whether in insect, animal, or man; something very sensitive to conditions outside the germ cell itself. Heredity has ceased to be the hard and fast thing that earlier Mendelism emphasized.

The socially minded biologist can say: Let those who cannot produce their own children observe the social insects even at their lowly level of instinct. The sterile individuals among the ants or bees, denied as they are any progeny of their own, will become foster mothers to the offspring of the queen. By this means the young of the insect community are tenderly nurtured. And so, the biologist as well as the sociologist will ask: Are there not children who need the affectionate care that foster mothers and fathers can give? Are there not men and women who need adopted children?

Nature, so democratic that the qualities of human offspring are unpredictable and so variable amid unity that physical appearance and ability are never identical between members of the same family, seems to say to all parents: "You have a real job on your hands and if you would be efficient, follow my example of orderly development and co-operate with me." Nature expresses herself through biological parenthood; nurture, the really big task stretching over the years, demands a high order of socialized parenthood. Nature and Nurture are ever complements one of the other. Nature knows no "legitimacy" or "illegitimacy," but she has a beatitude for those who face reality: "Blessed are they who let facts displace fears."

3

Adoptive Parents

All sorts of people adopt children; their names are on the social register and on the relief rolls; they live in city and in country. They are in the professions, in business, on farms, and in the skilled and unskilled tasks of industry. Their motives may be almost as varied as their backgrounds. Some people move toward adoption with deliberation and well-matured plans; others jump into it from impulse.

Adoption should be seriously considered only after certain searching questions are answered. Will my motives stand the test? Is adoption something more than a passing whim? Am I capable of warm, steady affection? Do I really like children? Can I grow with a child, be flexible enough to meet his needs as he grows beyond babyhood? Have I the poise and control that will keep me from projecting myself and my ambitions upon a child? Am I content with my mate and with other family members who must live under my roof? Do I realize that children were never meant to be mere emotional outlets for adults and that a child should not be adopted as a means of resetting a badly fractured home life? Am I in the habit of seeing my undertakings through? Perhaps few people can answer an unqualified "Yes" to all these questions. True it is that not all own parents can measure up to such self-examination, but adoptive parents in general have a harder task than own parents since they must face all the common problems of parenthood and certain specific problems growing out of adoption. It would seem that an added measure of such qualities as steadiness, courage, alertness, and flexibility is needed by the adoptive parent.

Two basic principles in all successful parent-child relationships are these: (1) The child must be allowed to grow according to his powers in the direction of the goal that is best for *him*. A fine mechanic is far more useful than a poor minister, teacher, or doctor. (2) Parents themselves must grow, must refrain from forcing the child into the mold of their own ambitions. Some people, especially those who have attained wealth and high educational status, are in danger of being overconfident concerning what they can do for and with any child. Parenthood is a long-time job, not of pressures, but of guidance.

In view of the present population trend and the fact that most placement agencies have long waiting lists which amount to several applicants for each child, it is not surprising that the adoptive family is typically a one-child situation. Can a family take unto itself too many children? The answer, essentially the same for the adoptive as for the biological family, depends upon the motives in having children, and upon the mental, emotional, and financial stability of the adults. When an individual seeks to adopt some thirty children, as one tried unsuccessfully to do in North Carolina a few years ago, it can be suspected that a normal home is not assured. Also, if the taking of additional children means that some of them will not have all the rights and privileges of family life including inheritance, there is justifiably considerable question as to the propriety of such addition in the name of adoption. Too many children in a household may give it an institutional atmosphere with some likelihood that the individual child may get too little attention just as in the single-child family there is some danger that the child will get too much attention.

What are the marks of a "good" home? There are rules for building bridges, for raising chickens, and for painting pictures; and there are being worked out by specialists certain standards for a family that will afford a safe environment for a child, physically, mentally, emotionally, and socially.

The United States Children's Bureau, much interested in recent years in foster home placement as a means of caring for dependent children, has published a bulletin (*The A-B-C of Foster Family Care for Children,* no. 216, year 1933) intended as a guide for welfare workers engaged in home-finding for their young charges. In it are listed the "minimum essentials" which every child needs, "as much for the good of society as for the individual concerned."

There can be little doubt that the first indispensable is security, "a feeling of stability, and of belonging and counting for something in other lives." As far as can be determined, this is a fundamental requirement of all human beings but particularly of the child offered for adoption since he has already been uprooted from a home broken by death, by poverty, by discord, or in some other manner. While the need is largely emotional it must be met partly by material means. Hence, the financial ability of the foster parents must be considered.

A home of great wealth is not ordinarily desirable because there the child is less likely to have the close companionship and understanding of his elders. However, there should be enough regular income not only for the basic physical needs but also to guard against too much discussion of ways and means. More than one youthful tragedy has been induced by the fear or the conviction of the young person that he was a burden where the daily conversation of his home centered about money.

It is clear from the Children's Bureau publication just mentioned that if the home is to meet or exceed the "U. S.

Standard" (like the canned foods on its shelves), it must score well in the following physical, educational, social, and religious needs:

Adequate Shelter: a clean, light, well-ventilated, orderly home; properly heated in winter; with sanitary toilet facilities. The child should have a separate bed and a place in which to keep private possessions and to entertain friends.

Nutritious Food: there should be enough of it; it should be simple, well-prepared, and adapted to the age of· the child; it should be served at regular hours amid attractive surroundings, and eaten at leisure in a cheerful atmosphere.

Comfortable Clothing: clean, whole, attractive garments that fit and that are individually owned; sufficient changes for cleanliness; adequate protection against inclement weather.

Health Habits: individual toilet articles; frequent baths; proper care of teeth; regular bedtime and plenty of sleep; abundance of fresh air and pure drinking water; several hours of outdoor play each day; definite teaching of health rules and of wholesome, happy, courageous attitudes; sensible instruction in sex matters.

Recreation: a safe, clean, roomy place for outdoor and indoor play; suitable play materials and tools; sympathetic supervision.

Education: attendance at a community school of good standards as long as the law requires, and as much longer as the child's capacities warrant.

Vocation: development of each child's fullest capacities through high school, commercial, or trade school training in line with special abilities.

Family Life: a chance to live in a normal family group of differing ages without being crushed by numbers; to develop mutual attachments and a sense of responsibility for others and for the work of running a household.

Community Life: have a part in community group activities and festivities; opportunity to make friends in natural ways through entertaining and being entertained; normal neighborhood contacts and wholesome associations with persons of the opposite sex.

Morals and Religion: positive teaching of standards of right and wrong aside from measures of discipline; daily contact with adults of sound character and inspiring personality; attendance at religious services of the type preferred for each individual case.

The above list of "government specifications" is meant to be used for all foster homes both temporary and adoptive. While it may be difficult for the child-placing agency to uphold these standards, the task is simple compared to dealing with the adult incompetency and delinquency which result in a large number of cases from failure in the home. "A child should be deeply rooted; bound to his environment on every side by ties of interest, habit, and affection. Only so can he attain the stability to withstand the storms of later life and make his fullest contribution to society."

In a study of over nine hundred children, made several years after their placement, it was found that the primary condition of successful development lay in the kind of relationship which grows up between the child and his foster parents. "Undoubtedly the child's adjustment to his foster family governs to a significant degree his adjustment to society, and this family relationship had less to do with the standard of comfort and place in the community than with the human qualities and understanding of the family members." Some of these persons had married or were working away from home, yet the family bond remained so close that many of these older ones as well as of the younger foster children had come to think of their parents' ancestry as their own.

The real test of the effectiveness of family life is met when cultural heritage is transmitted easily and naturally to all family members. In the records of 217 foundlings the unselfishness and pride of the foster parents are noticeable as over and over they say, "He couldn't have suited us better if he had been our own." Many of the children became so imbued with the characteristics of their foster families that they grew to look like them, took on their mannerisms and general appearance, and entirely measured up to the standards of the adoptive parents and their friends.

A wholesome parent-child relationship depends to a great extent upon the emotional adjustment of the parents to each other and to their world. In fact, an institution may be preferable to a home permeated with emotional tensions and discord. If the adopting parents have been childless for several years, or have feelings of inadequacy for which they hope to compensate, the danger of strain in the family situation will be considerable. Because most children available for adoption, unless they were taken in extreme infancy, have had deprivations and insecurity, it is to be expected that there will be some loss of that emotional stability so necessary to concordant living individually and socially.

The presence of emotional difficulties in the would-be parents, unless very serious, need not permanently discourage them from seeking a child, but these difficulties should be taken into consideration. A home that crushes one child may be stimulating to another of different age, sex, or temperament, or better suited to several than to a single child. On the other hand, some families financially able to bring up three or four children may be emotionally incapable of integrating more than one. In most instances the taking of the child should probably be postponed until the problems can be adjusted or improved, sometimes a simpler matter than at first appears. They may need the intervention of a mental hygienist, physician, or psychiatrist; but seemingly insuperable difficulties sometimes resolve themselves after a rest or change of scene during which perspective is gained and courage recovered. It may be that minor rather than deep-seated tensions are caused by the presence of some relative, especially in crowded households. No child can be or should be an antidote for a poisonous family situation; but the home with a reasonable interflow of affection and a reasonable degree of emotional ups and downs is better for the child than the colorless, flat regimentation of the average institution.

If the emotional disturbance is caused by marital friction some compensation other than adoption should be sought. Every child needs two parents working in harmony for his good. If the couple is unable to react to each other on an adult level of sportsmanship and loyalty they will be unable to act together in the crises that demand a united front of authority or of unselfish devotion. Parenthood is no more a panacea for a disappointing marriage than marriage is a cure for a personality at war with itself.

In any family relationship the age factor is of some significance. Records indicate that adoptive parents average ten or more years older than biological fathers and mothers, that is, they are in the thirties, forties, or even fifties at the time of taking the child. This may be in part because they have been hoping for own children; because they were both engaged in professions that would suffer by interruption; because the earnings of both were needed; because of ill-health, living with relatives, or for various other reasons, not forgetting those who indicate that children would curtail their freedom or interfere with their plans. (Indeed the latter may have considerable long-run usefulness in humanity's interest, for people too self-centered to want children are possibly too selfish to make good parents.) Whatever the cause, the majority of adoptive parents are of mature years. They themselves are the first to say that this is in some respects a handicap, as the years leave their mark in loss of mental flexibility and physical strength. But older parents may, on the other hand, have learned tolerance and patience, may be more leisurely. Financially, professionally, and socially they may be better established. Mental and social age, emotional maturity and balance count for more than calendar age.

The childless couple approaching the middle years see life slipping behind them and feel that something has been missed, or they wish to share the comfort and position they have achieved. Will adoption enrich their lives and give to some child a real chance at growth and happiness? Have they the physical margin of safety that will enable them to companion and care for the child with serenity and judgment? (How many foot-pounds of energy are consumed by an hour's play or a day's supervisory contact with an active two-year-old!) Can they reasonably expect to live long enough to see their child through his educational program, and avoid burdening him too early with their old age? As for this last point, the emotional dependence of the elderly is with few exceptions a load for their children at times, even when not complicated by the need for financial assistance. Unless the answers to such queries are in the affirmative, probably some other satisfactions should be looked for than those offered by child-rearing, unless an older child is acceptable. "Had the idea of adoption crystallized a few years earlier, how different things might have been," some are forced to sigh in resignation.

To forestall such frustration, people would do well to make at least tentative plans at an earlier age, in view of the fact that the waiting period after application for a child has been made is often months or even years. There is no reason to hesitate on the grounds that a child may yet be born. Experience goes to show, in homes where there are both own and adopted children, that in most cases the adopted child is as much loved and returns as much affection; that he is as well adjusted and takes his full share of family responsibility; that his parents' feelings and attitudes toward him are no different than toward their own.

To another type of couple adoption affords great satisfaction because it overcomes an inadequacy and assures normal family life to people otherwise deprived of it but capable of prizing it highly. For a number of years changing social attitudes plus a fairly satisfactory technique of contraception have permitted many marriages of people who, for reasons of personal health or unsafe physical or mental inheritance are not fit candidates for parenthood. Their homes have the flavor of purposive forethought, self-control, and acceptance of life on its own terms that are ideal for child-nurture. There is no reason why their doors should not be opened to homeless babies early in their marriage, as soon as their adjustments to each other are made, thus giving themselves and their children the benefit of practically complete family experience. It should be added that in such cases sterilization of the deficient partner may be desirable in order to free the adopting parents from the fear and the danger of pregnancy. The child will need his mother's full strength for two or three years, unimpaired by illness or worry; he will need from both father and mother the serenity that comes from unhampered, full sex expression.

The adopted child may do more for the erstwhile childless couple than merely to add his presence. The affectional interflow between all three may set in motion reproductive forces hitherto inactive and powerless. Some years ago an experienced superintendent of a children's home society was heard to say: "I've noticed quite often that a childless wife will give birth to one or more children fairly soon after she and her husband have adopted a youngster." This "hunch" seems to have some support in a study of 273 cases of adoption by H. F. Perkins in his article, "Adoption and Fertility." In each of 200 of these adopting couples where pregnancy had never occurred, at least one child was born within an average period of 38.8 months after adoption and approximately within ten years after marriage. It would seem that the three-point relationship, with its new bonds and stimulations, does something to awaken dormant reproductive powers.

No discussion of adoption is complete without mention of the unmarried foster parent. Sometimes the bachelor woman who does not expect to marry and who has an established income eventually longs for a child. For her, two questions arise in addition to those faced by all aspirants to parenthood. Should the task be undertaken single-handed? Will a one-sided home be fair to the child?

Only a very courageous person will say "yes" to the first. The responsibility of providing support in case her income fails, of planning unaided all the details of her child's life, of watching alone at the bedside on black days and nights of illness, of constantly being "on duty" as two persons at once, where two parents give each other relief by alternating their roles, to say nothing of intricate emotional problems arising from her single estate and from her child's lack of the balancing factors of a father's influence—all these may well give her pause.

As to the other question, will the fatherless home be a safe one for the child? Each case requires an individual answer. In general a child needs two parents, and it is no solution for two women to undertake the task jointly as is occasionally done. Many agencies will refuse entirely to place a child in such a home; in fact some go so far as to refuse to consider any but the orthodox, two-parent family. Only an exceptionally vigorous woman can carry the double burden, and at the same time maintain for herself an extra-familial life, interesting and stimulating enough to keep her from projecting herself upon the child and crushing his independence, or losing her perspective and exaggerating his importance. Yet occasionally it may be a successful venture if the woman has in her make-up a generous share of the so-called masculine qualities (not meaning the non-feminine, swaggering type that affects masculinity), if she is well adjusted, if she has brothers or other male relatives who will enter into the child's life, and if she has many outside contacts and interests. It may well be that one good parent is preferable to two mediocre ones. The well-to-do woman may find that adopting two or three children perhaps of both sexes may be safer than concentrating on one alone.

It is natural in undertaking any project to inquire: "How much will it.cost?" Hard as it is to put human growth and development into dollars and cents, some tentative estimates can be made. To begin with, it should be understood that there is practically no expense involved in the adoption process itself. In fact, in most states it is illegal to make any charges for services in connection with it except such incidental fees as may be incurred in copying records or looking up data. Many a foster mother laughingly tells her friends that adoption is much cheaper than bearing a child.

The cost then, of an adopted child is just what would be involved with an own child, deducting the expenses connected with birth. That may be roughly estimated as the same amount budgeted for any member of the family, whatever the economic level. As long as the baby's consumption is largely confined to milk, orange juice, and cod liver oil, this estimate may seem unduly generous, but the growing child has an amazing capacity for spinach and shoes, to say nothing of dental and medical care. Also the number of preventive inoculations and other prophylactic treatment grows yearly, even if illness is averted.

Unless children have been a definite part of the family program, it may be necessary to move to a larger house, to have more yard space, to go to a different neighborhood, or to be near a better school. The thoughtful prospective parent as he looks ahead to the time when his child, as a young man or woman, will have to leave home for further education, realizes that there will be a short period when the expense will be much heavier. This may be supplemented by the son's or daughter's earnings, with considerably less likelihood in the case of the daughter. Few parents, however, will intentionally handicap their child in an increasingly competitive world with the necessity for earning an education. Such a handicap involves the danger to the child of imperiled health, inadequate training, and the acceptance of a square peg, round hole expedient. This may mean the postponement of professional or business establishment and be accompanied by the hazards of delayed marriage or of mismating.

It is scarcely too much to say that adoption should not be undertaken by anyone whose prospects do not warrant the education of the child—according to his abilities—at least to the degree expected in that particular family. The best-laid plans of parents and others sometimes fall short of the mark through no fault of their own. But it is hardly fair to take a child for adoption with no reasonable expectation of fitting him for decent self-support.

Who, then, should adopt? The good citizen and the good neighbor, the self-supporting and the forward-looking, who can understand and love the child; those who are willing to prune away what might be considered less important interests, those who have not become dry and stiff in spirit but in whose trunk and branches there are the vitalities of growth into which young life can be grafted with prospects of enrichment and fruitfulness.

4

Steps in Adoption

"We want to adopt a child, but we don't know where to begin. How should we go about it? What are the first steps to take?" Over and over such questions are voiced to those who have a professional interest in child welfare and the family. Too often plans and hopes for adoption fail because the seekers do not find a suitable child immediately, and they become discouraged by the real or fancied risks and difficulties. To some there seems to be an undue amount of red tape which they resent as an interference with the strictly personal intimacies of family life.

This chapter aims to tell briefly and simply what are the necessary steps. Let us assume that you, the reader, are a prospective adopter. Perhaps you will be surprised to find that adoption is easier than you had supposed, easier than many less important transactions. The few requirements and formalities imposed do not arise from an unjustifiable snooping of the state or the public welfare department into your private affairs, but from the responsibility of the state to safeguard its homeless children from exploitation and abuse, and to protect its well-meaning but uninformed citizens from hasty decisions and neglect of legal forms.

There are several possible ways of finding a child but the one that offers you the most security with the least effort is to apply to a reputable child-placing agency. Your

state has one or more such organizations and many cities
have municipal agencies which meet modern standards.
Some of the persons qualified to advise you about the choice
of an agency are a state or local public welfare or child
welfare official, or a social worker concerned with family or
child welfare. In addition to the state agencies some regions
have excellent private agencies or adoption nurseries, but
before applying to a private placing bureau it is very important to make sure it is licensed by the state and has high
standards of professional work and personnel, because there
are in many states disreputable agencies with no concern for
children or for adoption, organized solely on a money-
making basis. Probably the nearest agency will serve you
as well as any other. Some people seem to look upon distance as a check to the intruding curiosity of certain acquaintances, but any such reticence should be weighed
against the practical considerations of the expense and in-
convenience of travel, the greater difficulties of investigation,
of possible legal involvements arising from nonresidence if
you go to another state, and in the case of small babies, of
changes of climate, of altitude, or other conditions of physical environment.

You have, let us suppose, decided to ask an agency to help
you select a child; perhaps you have made an appointment
for that purpose. Do not be surprised if you see no children
on your first visit. After a little talk about the kind of child
you think you would like you will probably be given a
blank to fill out, and asked for an appointment with a
field worker who will call at your home. These are the
preliminaries that will save your time and bring you to a
more satisfactory goal than you are likely to reach without
such help. The questions asked are as much a matter of
routine and as confidential as those you have met in a
hospital or doctor's office. However personal they may seem

to you they are just a part of the day's work to the receiving secretary.

Some of the information sought by the questionnaire or the field worker may concern the following: your religious affiliation, since some states and many child welfare agencies require that a child be placed in a home of the same religious faith as his natural parents; the health of your household, to protect the child from transmissible disease; your financial ability, not only as an indication that you are able to support a child but also as a guide to the type of child that will fit into your home. It is unfortunate that well-to-do applicants are sometimes reluctant to give information freely, since a child has to meet more demands in a home of wealth and social position, and so must be chosen with the greatest discrimination. If doors are not freely opened to the placing agency it will be handicapped and unable to give its best service.

The factual information on the application blank can supply only a part of the picture of your home. The field worker will help you check up on the fitness of your house for a child, not only in such practical matters as sleeping accommodations and play space, but she will, after a visit to your home, sense something of such intangibles as family relationships and traditions. Some adopters think of a child in terms of high achievement later on; others are content to adventure through sheer affection for a young life upon whom they project no dreams or ambitions. Even your imaginings of what you would like your child to be may be of value to the placing agency or social worker in helping you to find the child who gives some promise of developing according to your dreams.

You may have to wait for a few months before the agency finds a child that approximates your wishes or fits your home situation. A child that seems promising may have to be withheld until adequate physical and mental tests can be made, or until legal consent can be secured. Many times a delay that seems unjustifiable to the applicant arises from precautions that are being taken for his benefit and future happiness. Moreover in some parts of the country there are several applicants for every adoptable child, and this seems likely to continue or increase, with the laws and social work practice requiring more pre-adoption investigation which will make adoption safer and more satisfactory because many children formerly considered adoptable are now being permanently institutionalized. The waiting period will be less if you have been fairly flexible in your requests, at least in nonessentials. A long look down the years will aid perspective. One couple who asked for a six-months-old girl decided after some delay to accept a six-year-old boy. Before the final decree was granted a baby girl became available but the parents were already too much attached to the boy to give him up, and had come to see that he was more suited to them than a younger child would have been. Many applicants, at first impatient to begin their parenthood experience, have come to look upon the interval as an opportunity for much needed training without which they could scarcely have undertaken the task of child-rearing. Particularly if you have never had the care of children you will find a few weeks or months of preparation none too much, and you will be an unusual parent if you do not find child-study a fascinating pursuit.

Imagine now that at last the agency has a child ready for your inspection. You will be grateful for its skilled guidance in arranging this first meeting if the child is a year or more old. If there is any choice, the first interview should not be in an office since this is an artificial situation for all the participants. A better setting would be an environment to which the child is accustomed, whose familiarity will give him confidence and naturalness. Whatever the background, it may be desirable for you to play the role of a stranger only casually interested in the child. If he is aware of being under special observation he cannot be himself and may, under tension, exhibit behavior totally unlike his usual conduct, or he may react unfavorably to you if the situation has too great an emotional content. The small child clings to familiar ground and must be transplanted very gently, especially if his security has already been shaken by previous experiences.

Naturalness in meeting and getting acquainted can be arranged. The social worker who took the boy and girl, both prospective adoptees, to the theater where they were seated immediately in front of the prospective adopters, was a good strategist. Scrutiny by the interested pair of adults was possible during the performance. At the close, greetings of "surprise," and introduction of children and adults followed by a very casual invitation to dine together —all a part of the plan but with the children still unaware.

As for the toddler, here too some planning will insure naturalness. A little one, under consideration by a couple from a distance, was afraid of strangers and the would-be parents agreed to follow the lead of the wise social worker. Their coming was timed to fit the child's schedule, after a nap or feeding when she was at peace with the world. She was led by the nurse into a room where the mother-to-be sat talking with another member of the household. No notice was taken of the baby whose attention was diverted by the nurse. After playing for several minutes the child went toward a ball which had been rolled near the stranger who smilingly returned it. Another half hour of play gave an opportunity for mutual observation; then the nurse walked slowly out of the room, leaving the door open. The child watched her go but made no move to follow. After a minute or two she toddled toward the visitor who smiled but still made no advances. Her patience was finally re-

warded by the little girl's laughter and uplifted arms. At
this point the nurse returned with orange juice and in the
absorption of drinking it the little one seemed hardly aware
that a man (her prospective father) had entered. For him,
the original procedure was very nearly duplicated but considerably shortened. In little more than an hour from the
time of their arrival the shy child who so often cried at
strangers had made definite and happy approaches to both
new parents.

The following day the mother in the background observed
the child's meals and routine care such as bathing and
dressing. An automobile ride, accompanied by the nurse
in order to ward off any fear of strangeness, was part of
the program. On the third day either the father or the
mother was with the little girl constantly and assisted the
nurse in her care. The next morning found parents and
child started happily on their homeward journey.

With a still younger baby, or with one who is less observing or less fearful, the introduction can be made somewhat
more quickly and easily. So also it may be shortened in
the case of a child old enough for explanations. But however long it takes, it should not be hurried, for all who
deal with children understand that their tempo differs from
that of adults. Time should be given, not only for the
parents to make up their minds but for the child to accept
them. The ideal is mutuality, with the child enabled to
make some choice, or at least allowed to accept or reject
advances. Naturally he cannot be expected to choose intelligently but his emotional reactions deserve respect.

Personality shows itself at a much earlier age than is
commonly supposed, and all children do not prove equally
desirable. However, due allowance must be made for un-
attractive clothes and haircuts or unfavorable surroundings.
Those who work with children know well the seeming miracles wrought by care and affection in a few weeks' time,

and there is no need for discouragement if you do not feel immediately and strongly drawn to the child tentatively chosen for your consideration. Closer acquaintance may reveal unsuspected charms. On the other hand, sophisticated people well beyond the "romantic age" have been converted to a belief in love at first sight by some small person with a winning smile.

It is important, since smiles are not wholly reliable, to take time to read and consider thoroughly the records that are available. These should tell what is known of the child's biological parentage and the circumstances of his commitment. Their value as a guide to choice is largely in your mental attitude toward them. If they seem of minor importance or if they inspire you with greater interest in and sympathy for the child, the venture is probably a safe one. But if they shock you or make you feel that he is any less worthy, any less your equal as a person to be respected, it may be wiser to delay action for a little. It is true that affection may become great enough to cover real or apparent defects in a loved one, but it cannot be depended upon to do so. In such moments of frankness as occur between those bound by close ties, fear or suspicion of failings due to bad heredity may slip off the tongue and smite the defenseless child. Your son or daughter has a right to your good faith and to your support and protection against all the world. If you feel any threat to your wholehearted acceptance of a child by reason of his ancestry or early experience, your procedure must then be cautious.

The records also may show the reports of doctors and psychologists as to their estimate of the child himself. Your agency will not offer you a defective child but he may have peculiarities that should be taken into account. Occasionally successful placement is made of a sickly child with a doctor, nurse, or nutritionist; or of a retarded child with a teacher or psychologist. Such a task is a challenge to the parent and a boon to the child. There can scarcely be a finer and more rewarding undertaking. However, for the average parent a normal child makes enough demands. The requirements of special care would be likely to hazard the relationship and risk the child's well-being.

Nor should you be discouraged if you fail to find the right child at first. The decision will be one of the most momentous in your life and deserves, therefore, patient and thoughtful consideration. Of course, you are not looking for the Perfect Child. If he were found he would be a misfit in most homes! If your desires are reasonable you should be able to find in a few months or at most a year or two, a child to whom you can give your affection and make the heir to your traditions, though he may bear little resemblance to the child of your dreams, as is true of own children so often. If the quest and request still seem to fail, another agency may be approached, or possibly you should scrutinize your home in the light of a child's needs. Is there any factor to make the agency hesitate to help you in your search? Remember that its appraisal includes much more than adequate housing and ability to support. It takes into consideration the disposition and relationships of family members and their philosophy of life. In most parts of the United States the demand for children to adopt exceeds the supply, which means that some delay is inevitable, especially if your home is one where only a child of superior endowment could fit promisingly.

You have made a tentative choice of a child, let us say, and now you are ready for the next equally important step, that of legal procedure. Adoption is an artificial process, legally speaking, hence it is necessary to carry through every detail exactly according to statute. All states have adoption statutes which follow a general pattern though with considerable variation in particular items. Again the placing agency or child welfare department will advise as to the requirements in your state and will help in many ways to explain and to meet them.

Your first legal move will be the filing of a petition in the proper court. The petition will probably be a standard form furnished by the court or welfare agency, to be filled in with such information as your name, residence, occupation, perhaps your age and reasons for wishing to adopt; name, age, address, and sex of the child, and the new name by which you want him to be known; names and residence of the child's natural parents if they are known or a statement that they are unknown to you. Again the agency will help you to secure the consent of the child's natural parents or guardian in the manner designated for your state. The court will appoint the time and place of the hearing, which may be as brief and informal as an interview in a business office, with only the judge and petitioners present, or it may be in the courtroom with the natural parents or guardian present, and possibly the child. In any event the hearing will be conducted with dignity and privacy and will probably take only a few minutes of time. In the states that require a period of trial residence there may be two visits to the court. At the first you will be given a temporary order for the care and custody of the child, but not until the final decree is granted is the adoption complete.

Supervisory calls by the agency representative are likely to be of value to all types of homes in such matters as adjustment between child and adoptive home, relatives, and community situations. No matter how advantaged the home, supervisory visits should be welcomed for the objective suggestions that can be given. A biological mother usually needs guidance in the first months; even more so may the adoptive parents need counsel during the trial period which usually ranges from six months to a year in progressive states. Indeed, all adoptive parents, rich and poor, should be thankful when their state and its social agencies consider the child's welfare so seriously that periodic visits are in the legal and social order of things. Even though the state does not require such check-up, the trial period should be advised as it often is by agencies in states where the law remains inadequate at this point.

The decree may be a standard form giving pertinent information, similar to that in the petition, or it may be a confirmation by the judge of the agreement which some states require the petitioner to make, to the effect that he will bring up the child as his own, giving him proper care and education, or it may be some other designated style of document. Some courts give the adopters a copy of the decree, others consider their records sufficient evidence.

The placing agency or child welfare department will help you to make sure that all records are correct, including the changed birth registration, and to get a copy of a new birth certificate for the child, if your state makes that provision. In some states a new birth certificate is issued whose wording does not reveal his original name and parentage, but only his new name with date and place of birth and perhaps the names of the adopters as parents. In other states the names of the adopters together with a note about the adoption is added to the original certificate. Whatever the prescribed form, one of your first responsibilities as a parent will be to obtain a copy of this certificate for your child. The bureau of vital statistics will furnish it at no expense other than a small fee for copying.

After the final decree has been granted the child is yours as irrevocably as if he had been born to you. No power can take him from you so long as you provide for him and treat him as your child, if statutory requirements have been met. He takes his place in your family as an own child in all respects except that of inheritance, about which in some states there are some restrictions.

The adopted child can usually inherit from his adoptive

parents without question, with exceptions in some states of certain kinds of property, usually land, which must descend only to blood kin. Inheritance is greatly complicated by moving to another state from that in which the adoption took place because of possible differences of state laws concerning property and additional difficulties in establishing the validity of the adoption. Complexities also arise over property owned in another state. Only a few states allow inheritance by the adopted child from adoptive relatives other than parents, that is, from adoptive grandparents, uncles, and others. Children adopted by the same parents or born and adopted children of the same parents usually share equally in the parents' estate, and inherit from each other as brothers and sisters. Still another difficulty where inheritance is concerned, in many cases, is the validity of the adoption. Records are scrutinized and if there appears to be any evidence that all requirements of the statutes were not complied with, or if the evidence fails to show compliance, the adopted person's rights may not be upheld. With so many possibilities of impediment to full rights of inheritance another parental duty, which the adopter will do well to exercise at an early date after the final decree is made, is to protect his child's patrimony by a will or trust fund in which the child is mentioned by name or otherwise clearly designated.

This chapter has so far outlined the easiest method of adopting a child with the help of an authorized child-placing agency. You may dispense with such services if you wish, but you will need to be doubly watchful of all details if you decide to handle them unaided. Adoption is a many-sided venture which often requires the aid of several professional skills to assure complete satisfaction and protection. Frequently a child is recommended by an interested friend who is perhaps a minister, lawyer, or physician, and it may seem simpler to accept his suggestion than to make a formal application to an unknown and impersonal agency. Or you may know of some child whose case has engaged your sympathy or whose parents have been known to you or have some claim upon you. There can be no objection to this more personal choice of a child, provided you feel under no more obligation to keep him, after a reasonable acquaintance, than you would feel if he had been a stranger offered by an agency for your approval. Adoption is such an intimate relationship that each adopter should make his choice freely, with due regard for tastes and feelings. The mature person will not be swayed by sentimentality but he will recognize differences in types of personality. Bobbie may be delightful, with a perfect health record, yet the fact that he is the child of an acquaintance or recommended by the friend of a friend does not prove that he is the child you want. As has been pointed out in an earlier chapter, parenthood has its emotional side, and some weight should be given to attraction, the strong surge of feeling that often surprises novitiate parents. Once you have decided on a child you will want to assure yourself of his probable mental capacity and health, and of your compliance with all legal requirements.

Especially is it important with the preschool child to make sure that sufficient mental testing has been done, particularly if the child's heritage is unknown. One test is hardly ever a safe guide; several developmental tests carefully compared and interpreted by a qualified psychologist are to be desired, at least if you expect your child to be able to do college and professional work. If the latter is your aim, it is not enough to demand a "normal" child, for the norm is far below your requirements. Only a definitely superior child will satisfy your wishes, and overplacement is as risky for him as for you. What most of us desire in our children is successful adjustment, whether that means the white-collar position or the overall job. A child cannot develop freely if he feels that he is never quite able to measure up to the heights set for him. As we have said elsewhere, the appearance of the child is not to be trusted. Many children unable to finish elementary school are sweetly attractive during their first years. In fact they may be far more appealing than bright children who have been mishandled. A sparkling eye and a ready affection may curtain a very dull mind. It is hardly too much to say that a pretty and docile child is a dangerous choice since doll-like prettiness is not likely to last and sometimes accompanies physical frailty. Docility is seldom if ever an asset quality.

Similarly the health of the child needs careful scrutiny by a doctor. Laboratory tests should be given to rule out the possibility of venereal disease which might later result in physical, mental, or nervous breakdown. If no definite abnormality can be found but if the general condition is poor, or if there is need of corrective treatment, such as tonsil and adenoid operations or special diet, it may be advisable for the child to be placed in a hospital or a special boarding home for a short period of physical adjustment before permanent placement is made. Not only does the average person, perhaps unused both to illness and to children, lack the special skills necessary to such care, but the restrictions and regimentation might well put too great a strain upon the developing relationship. A sick or convalescent child presents unusual problems at best and may well prejudice against him any but those deeply attached to him or those accustomed to the behavior of illness. The routine of a sick room with its new rules and deprivations sometimes makes a child rebellious against an adored parent whom he has long been conditioned to obey. Launching of child and parent into a new relationship, if adoptive parents and child are strangers to each other, calls for the best possible tension-free conditions.

The first legal point to determine is the proper court

where you should file the petition; first, what kind of court, second, where it is located. In most states adoptions are handled by courts having jurisdiction over probate matters, or by courts of general jurisdiction. The statutes of each state designate the court by name, and specify in what county or district it must be. It is usually the county or district where the petitioner has legal residence; in some states it may be where the child resides, or occasionally "where he is found," or where is located the institution having custody of the child.

The next step, after the petition is filed, is to secure the relinquishment of the child or consent to his adoption. Proper consent is fundamental to the validity of the adoption. You will need to know who are the persons qualified to give consent, and the required form of consent in your state. Generally both natural parents must give consent, or the mother if the child is illegitimate. If the parents are incompetent, have been deprived of civil rights, or cannot be found, most states provide for consent by some other person, next of kin in the state, legal guardian, person or institution having custody of the child, next friend appointed by the court, or someone else. In some states an adoption notice must be published in a newspaper if the parents are not found or the consents are not given. In some states the consenters must appear in person at the hearing, in others they may send their written and verified consents to the court. A few states require that the consents be attached to the petition or that the consenters join in an agreement with the petitioners, and a few allow a signed and verified relinquishment to stand in place of consent. It is not enough for the natural parents to say that they relinquish the child, not enough to make a written statement to that effect. Consents must be obtained from the designated persons in exactly the manner specified in your state.

In some states if the child was not placed by an agency

the court will make its own investigation by a probation officer or someone appointed by the court or by a public welfare official, of the fitness of the child and of the proposed home.

After the final decree is granted you are within your rights to request to see the records, to make sure that they are correct. States differ greatly in the matter of record-keeping. Some states furnish a copy of the decree or a certificate of adoption in addition to keeping the records in a separate, indexed book and sending copies to the welfare department and the bureau of vital statistics for their permanent files. Others make no provision for records and such as the court sees fit to keep are likely to be well hidden in the unindexed journal of regular court business. You will want to obtain all the evidence of the adoption that your state supplies, and make a careful check of the records. Occasionally a case may have such involvements that for the sake of all concerned, records may need to be impounded with the utmost secrecy. Adoption in this country is relatively so new, and the statutes controlling it so varied, that infallibility should not be assumed, even of the courts. They will give better service and protection if they receive intelligent and courteous co-operation. They need all pertinent facts and should not be blamed for mistakes made because adopters or natural parents, overzealous for secrecy, withhold or distort some detail.

It may seem that these legal points are unduly stressed, but it must be realized that while adoption is socially and emotionally like the natural parent-child relationship, legally it is an artificial relationship and collapses if all the regulations are not carefully observed. In olden times man protected his helpless young with cudgel and spear; legal weapons may be less dramatic but modern society has invented them for the same purpose.

Once you are conscious of their importance you may check

the details of your case under the guidance of the court. However, to many people it is a justifiable expense to consult a trustworthy lawyer and the assurance of his professional guidance gives freedom from worry, even when there are no unusual circumstances. It need hardly be said that if your proceedings develop any unexpected entanglements, they should be put in the hands of a competent lawyer at once. You cannot assume that the transaction is legal because "it is right" or because it "ought to be."

Thus have been presented some of the precautions to be taken when the child of your choice has been recommended by some person known to you, whose integrity you do not question but who is a layman in child-placing. It should be obvious that you cannot afford to trust a stranger who may pose as a doctor or nurse or minister. There are glib salesmen of babies as well as of household gadgetry. One of their chief talking points is secrecy—your relatives, neighbors, and the community need know nothing about the details! The catch is that neither will you ever be able to find out particulars that may be of extreme moment; or that you may later find yourself involved in sordid perplexities. It is hard to understand why concealment seems so desirable to many adopting parents. It might almost be said that until they are ready to speak of it freely and naturally, at least to close friends and the proper authorities, it would be better to postpone action, for furtiveness indicates some hidden fear or conflict or lack of readiness, and parents should be mature and balanced persons.

The baby bootlegger probably will continue to do business until our states have achieved something like uniformity in the laws relating to child dependency, and until there is more consistency of public attitude toward illegitimacy.

The unmarried mother, approaching confinement in an exaggerated emotional state, can scarcely be blamed for hiding herself in some obscure dollar-minded place that advertises itself as a maternity home and promises to dispose of her baby, though she would be safer and more comfortable in one of the many licensed and approved "rescue homes" maintained by charitable or religious bodies. These last mentioned give skilled medical and nursing care combined with a program of character building and restoration of morale; here the babies are often unusually promising but are rarely adoptable directly since the license of such homes does not ordinarily permit child-placing; and, moreover, their policy is likely to emphasize the keeping of the child by the mother or her family. When retention of the child by the mother is not feasible, such a good maternity home usually turns the child over to a placing agency or other children's institution.

However understandable, though deplorable, may be the unconsidered decision of a distraught mother, there can be no excuse for adopters who deliberately patronize baby farms or nonlegal maternity homes. There they run the risk of selecting a child of unknown parentage who has never had proper physical care or habit-training, who has been exposed to venereal and other infections, and about whom there are no reliable records. Such adopters are not only responsible for many of the unsuccessful adoptions but they unwittingly perpetuate by their fees and their connivance in an illegal enterprise one of the black pages of American culture. The state, through its licensing and placing laws and its administrative practice, seeks to protect both natural mothers and children as well as adoptive parents. For their own safety, if from no higher motives, adopters should be at least as careful in their choice of a child as in the acquisition of a horse or a dog. Baby farms and newspaper advertisements are not promising sources for permanent family members, nor should any agency which seeks a payment of money be approached with full confidence.

One further point needs to be kept in mind in view of

what is now known from biological and psychological science. An adoption or nursery home may provide otherwise excellent service but may have in its policy such inflexible rules of secretiveness about the child's heredity that the adopter and the child himself may be at a disadvantage some day. The adopter, and the adopted child later, has a right to know whether the hereditary stream is reasonably clear, whether there are hidden hazards (Mendelian recessives) such as asthmatic and epileptic tendencies and even more serious latencies that may conjoin unfortunately in the child or children of ultimate marriage. In other words, the eugenically-minded adoptee moving toward his own marriage may want to know as much as he reasonably can in precourtship and courtship days, about his own and the possible mate's hereditary strengths and weaknesses. To shut off the possibility of such check-up by rigid rules is far from desirable.

To adopt a child is a matter of honor and good sense for all concerned. Overmuch concealment and self-consciousness are undesirable. You cannot be so confident of the success of the venture if you have not openly consulted the best agencies and made use of all the checks and aids at your disposal.

The Adventure Begins

An important date in your family history is approaching, and as before all great events, the world suddenly seems to stand still. According to your temperament, you want to run toward the day, or you yearn to set back the hands of the clock. You are eager to taste the joys and grapple with the problems of the new experience, or you remember longingly your orderly days and carefree nights.

The die is cast. From this day forward, for better or for worse, for richer or for poorer, in sickness and in health, this child is yours.

Suddenly new meaning attaches to those earnest discussions of food values, naps, and sandpiles that you had thought rather overemphasized by your friends who are already parents. You wonder if you can ever remember and carry out the bewildering details whose performance seems to be an accepted adjunct of your new responsibility. However habituated to routine your household may have been, the clock now becomes its most important item. New techniques, new schedules, new relationships fill to the brim the first absorbing weeks, that yet have overtones of far-off, divine events. Above the straining of vegetables the stars sing together.

And then the day comes when particular items fall into place as part of the daily round and the hours march in decent order instead of erratically hop-skipping. The beat-

ing wings of majestic fate resolve into comfortably paced
rhythm, and a small body fits into the curve of an arm with
effortless naturalness.

One adoptive mother describes her early treatment of the
little stranger she had chosen for her son as that of a guest
in the house. Perhaps no better start could be made because
that implies respect and equality and the desire for approval on the part of the hosts, as well as concern for the
happiness and well-being of the visitor.

No attempt will be made here to discuss the general subject of child-training. If you have never had the care of
children, the period of waiting may well be one of study and
preparation as is often the case with biological parents.
Books, magazines, and government bulletins are available
as guides to the physical care, the habit-training, and the
understanding of children. Some child-placing agencies
have special manuals which are distributed to foster parents,
and nearly all are equipped to give advisory services.

The needs of the chosen child are those of all children,
fundamentally, but certain aspects of his life are likely
to be exaggerated or in need of greater emphasis in proportion as his care and surroundings have deviated from the
normal or the desirable. If the child of your choice is an
infant, your problems will differ little if any from those of
natural parents. His requirements will be mainly on the
physical plane. His first social efforts will be reflections of
your smile, your gestures, your speech, your activities, and
it will not be long before your friends will tell you, laughingly perhaps, but truthfully, how much he resembles his
parents.

It cannot be stressed too strongly that the little child has
no greater need than that of security, and this need is increased for the adopted child in proportion as his roots have
been disturbed. Even if no memory remains of the event,
a broken home causes an upheaval in the lives of all its mem-

bers. If there has been a series of boarding homes or institutional experiences, at best there is uncertainty and lack
of confidence. There may be desperate fear of new situations, or hostility to strangers. One mother says that it
took her five-year-old a week of sitting wild-eyed on the
edges of chairs before he could relax and decide that she
didn't eat little boys. A three-year-old chattered to her
adoptive father but would not speak to the mother for several
days, and showed fear at the approach of any woman. A
sturdy toddler accepted his new parents cheerfully but
seemed apprehensive of his new home and cried lustily every
time he was left alone for an instant, until he achieved
greater speed of locomotion and could run after a disappear-
ing protector.

Sometimes a little later when home and parents seem
wholly satisfactory to the child, fear arises lest he himself
will fail to measure up, or in the case of a child from a home
broken by death or desertion, "What will become of me if
this mother or father disappears, too?" Such fears are seldom expressed at the time and can only be inferred from
behavior. The hidden fears of children expressed when they
become older, are sometimes amazing as to type and degree.
Appearance and early history may give no clue to nervous
conditions that can be alleviated only by patient and gentle
assurance. Adopted children who seemed to adjust readily
have later confessed to childhood terrors due to feelings of
insecurity or inferiority.

Some overt signals of distress are tantrums, quarrelsome-
ness, disobedience, refusal to eat, sleep disturbance, bed-
wetting, masturbation, thumb-sucking or nail-biting, lying,
stealing, or running away. While such signs of nervousness
will need treatment because they are disturbing to others,
none of them is very serious in itself and will disappear more
quickly if the emphasis is on building up affection, confidence, security, and self-control, rather than on tearing down

a habit that is largely unconscious until attention is fixed upon it. For the young child none of these acts has the moral significance that his elders too often attach to them, and most of them are occasionally practiced by the most carefully trained, well-adjusted own children. (As for the so-called "problem child," we are reminded of the remark, "wherever you find a little problem child, look for the big problem adult.") Such traits indicate nerves rather than depravity according to science and newer theology, and call for rest and relief from tension rather than for nagging discipline or corporal punishment. Unless the child has inherited an inferior nervous system, proper physical care and freedom from emotional disturbance will give him mental poise, once he fits comfortably into his new home, except for the occasional lapses common to all children.

Quiet acceptance of each day's happenings, no matter how unexpected; gentle ministration according to a fixed schedule; steady, sure affection free from gushing emotionality —these will do much to reassure the faintest-hearted newcomer. Some specific ways of tying him to his new home are by providing possessions for his exclusive use. A feeling of permanence, of "belonging" attaches to one's own bed, dresser, and toy box; to towels or a silver spoon marked with one's own name. A pet or a "cuddly" toy may relieve loneliness and develop a sense of responsibility. The older child may be interested in planting a garden or starting a bank account. Any plans looking toward the future of the family as a whole—work, play, travel, education—will serve to establish its bonds more firmly. Every child needs some regular tasks about the home, not only to develop responsibility but also to give him a more secure place in the family life. It goes without saying that such chores should be as pleasant as possible, always with an eye to their training value rather than as a means of getting disagreeable jobs performed. The child who has spent some time in an institution may rebel at the sight of a broom or garbage pail but delight in flower arrangement or table-setting.

One gentle, tractable girl ran away from a "comfortable" foster home where for her there was only discomfort in the endless scrubbing and polishing, much of which she felt was "made work" to train her out of the slovenly ways of her own mother. She found refuge in a more easygoing household where she cheerfully took over the hardest tasks to save the strength of the frail mother. For the first time in her life she had her own room and spent most of her small allowance on its furnishings. Neighbor children were invited to play with her and their parents soon began to remark about her growing attractiveness. There was no money for new clothes, but the invalid mother made over her own for the little girl "because I can't go out much anyway so I only need one dress." The tight, stiff pigtails were cut off and many an hour of satisfying conversation took place as the mother patiently coaxed into curls the hair that was now soft and shining from its introduction to soap and water. The father began taking the child to church, to movies, and on various outings, pleasures which he had largely given up during his wife's illness. The arrangement which was undertaken only as a temporary expedient ripened into a satisfying permanent relationship, marked by loyalty and continued interest though the child is long since grown, married, and established in a profession.

Next to insecurity, the homeless child probably suffers most from feelings of inferiority. He may have cause to be ashamed of his own family or neighborhood; he may have been taunted on the playground with being a "charity child," or an orphan, or illegitimate, all couched in vulgar language possibly unknown to the average adult. With a change of environment the child may become acutely conscious of differences in manners, in speech, and in dress which he is helpless to overcome. He is often undernourished and otherwise physically handicapped. He may have been so bullied and beaten that he stands in terror of anyone bigger than himself. Perhaps his former social assets were lying and stealing and fighting, and he is chagrined and puzzled to find that what was acceptable behavior in his first environment is taboo in the second. If he came from a haphazard family that never sat down together for a meal, that indulged in baths occasionally in hot weather and slept only when street attractions waned, he might well feel smothered by a moderately orderly household, however gently enforced its rules.

On the other hand, if he has been subjected to the regimentation of an institution for some time, he will face with bewilderment the comparative freedom of a democratic family and be unable to direct his own activities or fill constructively his unplanned hours. The sole complaint that a recently adopted boy made of his new home to a sympathetic friend was that "They don't tell me what I must do." This boy's situation is interesting for several reasons. With meal times occasionally changed for the convenience of the family, with home affairs so well managed that the work element was unobtrusive and accomplished with strange tools, with parents so considerate that they hesitated to criticize his speech or manners, he was excusably worried over his place as a family member. He was eager to conform but needed, nevertheless, a little direction and interpretation of unfamiliar ways.

The cowed and timid person is not the only sufferer from feelings of inadequacy. The noisy, blustering, impertinent child may be "showing off" to hide his hurt feelings or to gain attention from those whom he wants to impress. Nor does the inferiority necessarily exist. A fancied inequality may do lifelong damage and never be suspected as the cause of apparently unrelated difficulties.

Whether or not there is any noticeable reason for lack

of self-confidence, the wisest parents will not overlook any opportunity of cultivating it. This does not mean allowing the child the center of the stage or singling him out in any way. Quite the contrary, in fact, for what he most needs is to become an accepted and inconspicuous member of the group.

Perhaps the beginning should be made on his appearance. Comfortable clothes, suited to the occasion and in no way different from those of the children who will be his playmates, will go far toward giving him peace of mind. If he looks like the others in the group he may be accepted by them before they notice more subtle dissimilarity. And let no one think that clothes and styles of haircut are less important for the boy than for the girl. Any child, at least of school age, stands or falls in a new environment by the degree of his conformity to his peers and no parent ever quite learns the criteria of the other children. The wise mother will close the fashion books and refuse to be browbeaten by salespeople, at least until she has studied carefully the apparel of her friends' children. Father's advice may be worth heeding because he is likely to have fewer preconceived ideas of what the well-dressed child should wear. Hand embroidered garments can feel like a haircloth shirt if one's comrades are wearing overalls.

After the choice of clothes is made, the less said about them the better. A child's wardrobe may seem unduly expensive, especially when purchased all at once, and it is natural to caution the wearer about its care. But mending and laundry must be weighed in the balance with social adjustment. A tired mother who had begged her boy not to get his clothes soiled realized that he had paid too high a price for cleanliness when she overheard the taunts: "Tommy's a baby, Tommy's a sissy." Tommy's short legs were none too dependable and the playground had hills and valleys of scuffed turf. The only solution that he could

reach was to refuse participation in all active games. A
family council—father's perspective is so often an asset at
such sessions—worked out a new policy. Play suits were
bought that required no ironing and Tommy himself was
taught to wash them each day, not as a punishment but to
give mother more time to read to him.

At best, some habit-training will probably be necessary
to help the child to conform to parental standards. If habits
have not been formed it should be a relatively easy matter
to establish them. Retraining is always more difficult, because the wrong habits must be broken down before the correctional conditioning can take place. Much will depend on
the co-operativeness of the child, and it must be kept in
mind that the growth of confidence and affection is more
important than rapid progress in learning new ways.

Some parents try to avoid nagging by deciding each day
or each week on one habit that is to be stressed and then
shut their eyes resolutely to undesirable behavior of other
kinds unless it is actually dangerous. A written list of
desirable changes may clarify the situation. It need scarcely
be said that such a list should not be left where the child
can see it if he can read, nor should he ever be allowed to
overhear himself discussed. Only after the parents have
determined in joint session the relative importance of the
items, are they ready to face calmly their first task in trans-
mitting the family heritage of social usage.

It will easily be seen that good food habits should precede
table manners, that sleep and toilet habits outweigh syntax
and precise diction. Not all distinctions are so readily made,
but much there is that demands discriminating thought. The
one exception to make in our habit inventory, as based on
values, is the *annoying* trait. It may be wise to eliminate
early in the game any mannerisms or characteristics that
arouse undue antagonism, bearing always in mind that the
ultimate aim is a mutually happy and satisfying relation-

ship, and no emotions that might hinder it can safely be allowed.

One family that faced particular difficulties in table manners worked out this plan: Mistakes were overlooked at the morning and evening meals but at noon when the father was away, the mother patiently showed and explained the desirable techniques. The little girl was allowed to invite a guest of her own choosing for a meal at the end of a week of satisfactory progress. The father who had traveled widely, told as bedtime stories the eating customs of other lands. The promise was made that the child should be taken to a hotel to dine as soon as she could do it inconspicuously. One day each week during the training period it was understood that no comments would be made. Sometimes a picnic basket was carried out under a tree or the child had an attractive tray in her own room, to free her from constant surveillance.

A long step has been taken toward overcoming faulty habits when both parent and child look upon them as mere incidents, perhaps as accidents that might happen to anyone, like measles or stepping on broken glass. Obviously the child is growing up when such habits are conquered. The process may be quickened by the development of "credit qualities." Any skills or arts in which he can excel and which he enjoys will add to his prestige with the group and so to his self-esteem. And again let it be said that there is little danger of overdeveloping this sentiment.

What is commonly diagnosed as conceit is far more likely to be exaggerated compensation for an inferiority feeling; whistling to keep the courage up. If the accomplishment is one which can be used to advantage in the home, another link is forged. A child whose daily musical diet had been jazz and blues songs was retrained to sing grace at meals. A boy who loved color repainted some of the furniture and expanded with pride to hear his mother boast of it to a guest. A child's handiwork deserves respect for its meaning and purpose whatever its intrinsic value, especially if it is proffered as a gift. So much of the giver goes into the picture he paints that he may feel unworthy and his affection lightly esteemed if he finds the gift in the waste basket. This does not mean that living rooms should be adorned with shrieking blobs of color; but most houses have an inconspicuous corner where love's labor, however crude, may not be lost. The adopted child may never before have had anything of his own to give and will be quick to sense any lack of appreciation in the recipient.

Enough of the problems of transplanting have been suggested to indicate their individual nature. To an even greater extent than with own children there can be no formulae, no blanket rules of procedure. Each case must be studied on its own merits. Books, friends, and professionals may advise but in the last analysis there is no substitute for a personal grappling with the situation.

A student of family relationships in a rural locality in 1932 was surprised to find a frequent answer to a question about sources of help in bringing up children, to be prayer. Possibly the practice of such prayer attitudes as reverence, humility, confession of mistakes, and aspiration is as good training for parenthood as the prescriptions of the more sophisticated child experts. Determined fact facing is the first step in any case. Factors bearing most heavily upon the situation are likely to be the child's background, the ages of child and parents, the traditions and standards which the family desires to transmit to the child, the attitudes of relatives, friends, and community toward the adoption.

Detached intelligence alone cannot build an ideal parent-child relationship because the bond is primarily emotional. This is just as true, though not so commonly recognized, in adopted as in own families. The deep surge of affection, as intense in its way as romantic love, leaves awed and breath-

less the foster parents who had supposed such feeling to be
tied up in some mysterious way with biological kinship. The
chilling fear that clutches parents as they keep vigil beside
their sick child, the red anger that blazes in the meekest
father or mother if injustice or danger threatens their little
one—these emotional extremes are known by all true parents. Nor, alas, is there any monopoly on the lesser emotions of impatience, annoyance, and irritability. The most
devoted parent is not proof against them, nor is the psychologist who can explain so glibly their mechanism and natural
history.

Emotional wear and tear is part of the price of parenthood and there is no immunity for adopters. A foster mother
writes early in her experience of the advantages of adoption
because adoptive parents view their children with more objectivity, and hence are less likely to spoil them, less likely
to fail to take full responsibility for their faults, less likely
to become oversolicitous. If she were writing ten years later,
could she still boast of detachment? Probably not, after
her emotions become more deeply involved. Parents,
whether by blood or by law, belong to a "great fraternity."

Little can be said of a general nature about helping the
adopted child to fit into the community, important as that
adjustment is. Much depends on community attitudes, on
the status of the family, on the personality of the child, and
on his background. It goes without saying that the introduction should be made as naturally and unspectacularly as
possible. The chief concern should be the comfort and welfare of the child, rather than the curiosity of the neighbors.
The standing of the family is already established in the community and that place will not be affected by the adoption
very much, but the child has everything to gain or lose. If
parents will bear in mind the probable reactions of friends
and neighbors, they can formulate a policy regarding the
manner of telling the news and the number of details to be

given. The matter is too vital to leave to chance or whim. Prying questions may be met with dignified refusal to discuss matters of so personal a nature, or with the simple explanation that you have promised not to divulge them. If no concealments need to be made, so much the better.

Few adoptive parents report any lasting difficulty or embarrassment, and many are surprised and touched by the genuine interest, helpfulness, and respect of friends and acquaintances. Observers state that whatever his background, the adopted child soon is accepted according to the position of the adopting family in the community, especially if its members show pride and satisfaction in him.

The surest weapon that can be put into the hands of the child as he faces the world beyond his own door is the knowledge of his adoption. If he is old enough to remember another home, he will need to have his past experience explained and interpreted, not fully perhaps, but enough to give him security and to help him meet questions and remarks. The child adopted in infancy should be told as soon as he can talk, in simple and few words, as for instance: "How glad we are we picked you out!" Introduce frequently the idea that he or she was especially selected. Children understand much of the speech they hear long before they can reproduce its sounds. The word "adopted" or "adoption" can easily blend in with other polysyllables. It need convey no mystery. Thus may the child be guarded against the hushed and awesome references that occasional visitors make, for adults are prone to talk about a child in his presence. Small ears will catch the pitying or wondering, perhaps the taunting or laughing remark. Unless awareness grows with him, he may be keen enough to catch the implication of such remarks that he is somehow different, set apart, or possibly inferior.

It is useless to try to keep the child from knowing the facts or even to postpone the telling until he is old enough to be told the whole story. Too many cases are on record of young people growing up with the fear or the certainty that they were adopted, but never mentioning it to their parents. Such concealed knowledge must create a barrier and a lack of confidence as well as needless worry and repression. How much better to have it a matter of common knowledge, something to be spoken of as naturally as any other fact. The child will see nothing stranger in that than in all the other rather mysterious life around him. The average adult reads into the child mind so much of adultness that is not there at all. It may be a prop to his self-regard later if he can confidently assure an inquiring or jeering comrade that he *certainly is* adopted. His parents chose him while most people just have to take what nature sends to them.

The method of imparting the information need cause no sleepless nights. If the decision has been made the opportunity will come, perhaps in the most unexpected manner. It is usually better to take advantage of a chance question or comment that the child makes, than to set the stage elaborately, because the situation is thus less likely to be charged with emotion. Often in later years, parents and children are unable to remember how the subject was broached or when, because it came about so naturally and undramatically. Information should come in small doses, as the child indicates a readiness and need for it. If too much is poured into his ears at one time he may be bewildered or fatigued and hesitate to ask further questions when they occur to him.

The problem was solved for one worried mother on the morning when her little boy found in the cage the baby bunnies that he had been expecting. As he contemplated the changed contours of the mother rabbit, he inquired: "Mother, did I live inside you?" "No, dear," she replied, "but Johnnie and Jane lived inside their mothers like that. You see, no little boy or girl came to live inside me, and we

wanted one, so Daddy and I picked you out." Subsequent
conversation was about rabbits and it was not for several
months that the subject was renewed. Then one day, after
a shopping trip the father was asked: "Daddy, where did
you buy me?" No one knew what was meant until in a
moment the explanation came: "Mother told me that you
and she picked me out. Did I cost a great deal?" It was
pointed out that little boys and girls are too precious to buy
with money, but that they are sometimes given to people
who want them very much if there is no one to care for
them, and that they are then called adopted, which really
means chosen. Mother added that it might be better not
to boast about it but being really wanted so much as to be
especially selected was quite a distinction.

In transplanting a rose bush the task is only half done
when the young shrub is set down in the hole that has been
dug for it. It requires special feeding until it is thoroughly
at home in the new soil; it must be sheltered from hot sun,
shielded from harsh winds, protected from cold, pruned and
watered and sprayed. All garden enthusiasts know that
sturdy plants depend more on daily watchfulness than on
occasional expert attention. If the premature bud is not
snipped off or bugs and worms thwarted in the nick of time,
the finest flowering may be prevented. Transplanting human
beings is no less a test of devotion and sustained attention, a
task calling for mature powers of judgment and self-control
as well as for the specialized techniques of the expert.

6

The Adoptive Family

Parenthood affords for most adults the highest satisfaction and fulfillment. Watching and guiding the development of a child into a useful citizen is an absorbing and vital experience for mothers and fathers. Children bring to a family an emotional equilibrium, a means of self-expression, and an extension into the future.

Students of the family remind us that parents need the child as much as the child needs the parents, that being a father or a mother is a social experience without parallel or substitute. While experts admit that many parents are unwisely affectionate toward their children, they call attention to another angle of the family situation which must not be neglected, namely that of the unwelcome child and the one that receives too little affection. Such children are to be pitied as much as those smothered in parental love, and their parents, or those people who sidestep parenthood altogether, are often half-starved emotionally whether they know it or not. The modern family, certainly no more imperfect than our other social institutions, still answers human needs rather well. Its failures, and they are fewer than its successes, come about from the personality defects and inferior motives of its members rather than because the family institution itself is weak. While the home is outwardly different from that of former days it still offers mankind its rarest chance to enjoy the richness of intimacy and the indispen-

sable opportunity to secure through parenthood the most
maturing and socializing experience obtainable in life.

For both parents and children the habit of living peace-
ably and co-operatively together carries over into other activities. Industrial investigations have shown that attitudes
toward other people make or mar co-operation. The person
who gets on well with his family and enjoys its group activities is not likely to have difficulty in his business and social
life. The intense, concentrated fellowship of the home serves
as a basis for the understanding of those with whom the individual members have contact in their outside association.
Mothering and fathering involves not only financial support
and physical care but also the unifying and interpreting of
the child's experience, which in turn often brings parents
face to face with the formulation of a working philosophy.

Whether the family group has come together by chance
or by choice, by biological or legal means, its relationships
are largely a matter of attitudes and adjustments between
personalities. The best of the family chronicle type of fiction emphasizes this mutual action and interaction. Sugary
romanticism pales before the more adult view of family life
as a continuing force through generation after generation.
Individuals come into the family by birth, by marriage, and
occasionally by less regular means; they leave it by death
or divorce. The torch is passed on from hand to hand and
at the heart of the flame is the distinctive tradition of the
family, made up of combined attitudes and practices evolved
from years of give and take of ideas and affection. Each
member makes his contribution plus or minus, yet each is
shaped largely by the steady pressure of group standards.

The adopted child is as likely to take on the attributes
typical of his foster family as is the own child. He will
prove as effective a vehicle of social inheritance. From
adoptive parents and children comes ample testimony to this
observation. Does the child who can remember being home-

less, before his adoption, react more strongly to formative processes, try harder to conform to family standards, take more pride in being a worthy family member? Frequently older children who were adopted at an early age testify that they commonly think of their adoptive relatives and ancestors as their own. Over and over parents state that their children resemble their (adoptive) families in viewpoint, in characteristic manner of meeting difficulties or successes, and in other distinctive ways, even to the choice of a business or profession that has become traditional, or of religious and political affiliation. No need is there to labor these cultural points even for the arch-hereditist. Surely it can be said that the adopted child absorbs and transmits family traditions as well as the own child.

As the family needs children to continue its pattern, so do the individual adult members need contacts with the young, not only to fulfil their hopes and dreams but also for emotional satisfaction which is as real a need, though not so tangible, as that for food and shelter. Family function moves along with humankind itself, advancing from the purely biological to sociological considerations with emphasis on emotional balance and the ability of the individuals to make adjustments. This places upon the home the burden of "perpetuation of human achievement," and means for each adult member of the family the honest shouldering of responsibilities and the willingness to give himself whole-heartedly to the close contacts of the group, whatever the consequences.

There should be no inference that family life at its best is ever devoid of conflicts and tensions. There are bound to be clashes of personalities, of desires, and of aims; disagreements between the generations, between the marriage partners, between brothers and sisters; parents, grandparents, children, more remote kin, and in-laws are all involved. Perfect accord would denote either dominance and sub-

servience, or stagnation. The successful family recognizes
the validity and desirability of differences that may mo-
mentarily seem discordant but which resolve harmoniously,
at least by sundown or soon thereafter! Even rather raucous
dissonance may later be seen to contain the leading tone
that heralded a change of key which added richness and
depth to the developing theme. It does not appear that
family strife often arises over the fact of adoption, popular
fiction to the contrary. Out of sixty cases in one study only
two reported any disapproval of adoption or of the particular child adopted, by relatives. Perhaps the explanation may
be found at least in part in the assumption that adoption
would hardly be attempted in a family where serious opposi-
tion could be foreseen.

A study of 910 foster children (*How Foster Children Turn
Out* by S. van Senden Theis) several years after their placement indicates that the most significant factor in determining the future of the child was not the type of home into
which he was taken, but the kind of relationship that developed between him and his foster parents. One of the
wealthiest and best educated families completely bungled
the training of their adopted son, yet some of the plainer
homes with little money or education, showed remarkable
understanding of their children. About sixty per cent of
the children studied had developed satisfactory relationships
with their foster parents and had formed lasting ties comparable to the customary parent-child feeling. Another
twenty-five per cent formed temporarily successful foster
relationships. The outstanding fact in this survey of foster
relationships is that more than half of the children found
affection, confidence, and permanence which they had been
denied. A smaller group found, if not so permanent a relationship, at least a temporarily satisfactory one. They en-
joyed for a short time the sense of having a home, good
surroundings, and a feeling of fellowship. The relation-

ship can be assumed to have been equally satisfactory to
the parents, at least in the group in which it was permanent.
The study explicitly mentions that for both parent and child
the foster relationship often becomes a complete substitute
for the natural tie, especially when the child is adopted at a
very early age. Nearly all the children in this "successful
relations" group, as might be expected, turned out satisfactorily in their other affairs, that is, they were self-supporting
and made suitable adjustments in their social settings. Further data were not collected as to their adult interests, but
a placing agency report of a list of notable men and women
who were foster children mentions a justice of the Supreme
Court, legislators, mayors, bankers, physicians, college presi-
dents, clergymen, lawyers, and members of other equally
honorable and useful callings.

The many fortunate adoptions, successful from the view-
points of both adopted and adopters, do not prove that all
childless couples or lonely bachelors of either sex should
adopt children. There are probably some persons who hon-
estly dislike children. Still others, doubtless a very small
percentage, have personality kinks or twists so hard set by
habit that neither mental hygiene nor psychiatry can make
them safe for the young. Cer ainly there are those who are
too unstable emotionally, or too immature, or in too uncertain health to cope with parental problems. There are others
whose lives are so dedicated to some intellectual or scientific
pursuit that they can ill afford the interruptions of child
care. Yes, it must be admitted that there are people who
should never have children just as there are those who should
never marry. But for the majority of intelligent, well-
adjusted persons parenthood is such an enriching experience
that it is worth all it costs. There is no evidence that adoptive parents have smaller rewards than biological fathers and
mothers.

Parents and teachers are often heard to say that they learn

as much as they teach in their contacts with children. Thoughtful people acquire, as parents, a self-control and a self-direction that no other experience has taught them, when they realize to what an extent the child mirrors home attitudes and moods in his early years. His consideration of the rights of others depends more upon his family experience than upon precepts. He learns to get his way by strategy or by more direct methods, according to daily example. His notions of honesty and fair play follow parental patterns to a great extent. His attitudes toward authority, toward work, even his sense of humor show the daily influences that surround him. Parental growth also occurs as interests widen under the searching questions of an unfolding mind.

Again, partly as a result of a new "aliveness," partly in answer to growing needs or desires, greater attention is often given by parents to business or profession. To the uninitiated this may look like the drive of necessity, another proof of the burden that children impose upon their elders. Actually a good part of the motivation arises from increased interest in the job for its own sake. Parenthood is stimulating, mentally and emotionally, much like marriage, and this stimulation coupled with the "settling" and maturing process of acknowledged responsibilities sometimes inspires even the moderately endowed person to unexpected achievement.

A common demand of the conscientious parent is for the best possible living quarters. Mr. and Mrs. Jones may be content with second best for themselves, may prefer a good car or better clothes or membership in the country club. But at the appearance of Jimmie, whether his coming was presided over by the stork or by a judge, they begin to think of home in terms of a play yard or a street free from traffic. They are quite right, they are growing in socialization (a far cry from social snobbishness) and should not be dubbed social climbers because they suddenly demand a better neigh-

borhood. Next to his family, it will do most to shape Jimmie's life. His mind will be filled with conflict if there is
too much divergence between the standards of family and
play group, and the influence of the playmates may prove
the stronger.

As for the house, it is worth almost any budgetary feat to
have elbow-room. The demands upon the mother are greatly
reduced by adequate play space indoors and out, where the
child does not encroach upon the leisure or work of his
elders and where his piles of blocks and precious "collec-
tions" are not endangered by unheeding adults. Habits of
work that will last a lifetime may be acquired at a small
table with a low chair in a corner free from interruption.
All children have this need for a private life somewhat apart
from grown-ups, yet within sight or sound of a supervising
older person. The adopted child perhaps needs to a greater
extent his own "place" and his own "things" to build security and serenity. Parents also need some space and time
uncluttered by their children. To admit this implies, of
course, no lack of affection but rather promises a more permanently close relationship than that based on attempted
identification.

Jimmie is not only learning independence but is relieving
his mother of time-consuming tasks when low rods or hooks
and a small stool enable him to achieve at an early age the
ability to wash and dress himself. Child-size furniture is
not only more comfortable for Jimmie but it saves wear and
tear on the more expensive adult furnishings. It can be
made out of a packing box and a can of paint by any one
with a slight knowledge of the use of hammer and saw, and
even if the result is not wholly aesthetic it may have values
not to be found in the more standardized store product. One
wee fellow in diminutive overalls "just like Daddy's" learned
lasting lessons in co-operation as well as in the use of tools
when he "helped" his adoptive father build play equipment

and furniture which he and his mother later painted in colors of his choosing.

The argument is scarcely valid that it is not worth while to provide special equipment for the child because he will so soon outgrow it. The habits and attitudes that are formed before school days are his permanent stock in trade, and tools for their fashioning are swings and slides, stout shovels and small red wagons. Nor is their use as temporary as at first appears. The "jungle gym" that provides merely climbing exercise for the three-year-old will make a turreted castle or a ship at sea for a crowd of schoolboys. The sandpile means mostly dipping and pouring to the toddler but becomes the material for imaginative projects demanding planning and concentration by the neighborhood group three or four years later. The parents of one six-year-old supposed he had outgrown sandpiles and refused his request for a fresh supply of sand. In a few days he had provided his own by pushing wheelbarrow loads up a hilly path from a brook bed. For weeks he and two neighbor boys carried out extensive engineering plans as they built roads and rivers, dams and bridges. When they were about to be discouraged by the impermanence of sand construction they learned to make cement blocks after a little coaching by a co-operative father. Who knows but these little lads will be the architects and planners of tomorrow's more beautiful cities!

Although the home of today no longer gives the education and the training in skills that was once a part of its function, yet constructive parental attitudes toward learning may furnish intellectual stimulus. Willingness to answer questions, story telling, guidance in reading, encouragement in constructive play, nature study, all these have a bearing on the child's mental growth and at the same time help to bridge the distance in years, which is likely to be greater between adopted children and their parents than is the case with blood-bond families. And the parent who has not begrudged the time and effort to live for a few years on the child's level of mind and interests will find that in a surprisingly short time not only is the affectional bond strengthened, and the amount of shared participation greatly increased, but also his own horizons have been widened by a whole range of subjects which heretofore he had not the time or the motivation to explore.

As the years go on, parent-child intimacy may be expected to provide an abiding sense of security and an emotional tone. Shared recreational activities not only bring out such qualities as honesty, unselfishness, and good sportsmanship but also loosen tensions and provide relief from restraint and may be a regenerating influence to balance the more impersonal and sometimes discouraging contacts of the outside world. Just as the parent-child relationship is the first socializing influence that impinges upon the child, so is it the last fine flowering of full social stature for the parent.

The role of the child in the family is somewhat fixed even before his entrance upon the scene by the age of his parents, by the presence in the home of grandparents or other people, by his position in regard to brothers and sisters. Mr. and Mrs. Jones react differently to each other at forty than at twenty-five years of age, differently early in marriage than after many years of adjustment, and their attitude toward the child of their youth is bound to be unlike that toward the heir of their maturity, whether the child in question is own or adopted. Not only is the child "put in his place" more or less unconsciously by his parents, but also by his brothers and sisters. Much depends upon whether they are younger or older, and how great the age difference happens to be; also on whether his coming was expected or desired by the other children. Cousins, aunts, uncles, grandparents, and others on the periphery of the kinship circle come in for their share of influence. Yet no phase of family life is static, least of all its relationships. Members grow and mature physically, mentally, and socially; one or more of them travels, has a new job, loses his money, has a long illness. They take up physical culture or theosophy. A careful study made of a given family today and another made five years hence would yield very different results and both be equally true.

Not only do relationships change within the family but its personnel changes with the passing years. Children grow up and marry, either to leave the parental roof or to add a new member to the household. Work or a better opportunity calls away first one and then another, perhaps permanently.

The door can never be locked against Death, and it is within the four walls of the home that bereavement is felt with almost intolerable poignancy as lifetime habits are broken. Then the whole situation must be redefined and new responsibilities must be assumed by each member. Thus we see a gay, irresponsible girl become her father's dependable companion as she tries to fill her mother's place. A less fortunate adjustment results when the remaining parent overcompensates for his loss by a managing domination that frustrates the young person in his desire to achieve higher family status. Be it noted that in times of crisis as in the more normal and everyday conditions of home life, the adopted child makes an excellent showing. Cases have been reported where the adopted child assumed the care of aged foster parents even though there were own children who might at least have shared the responsibility. One mother chose to make her home with her foster daughter though her own children were able to support her. A married foster daughter left her home to care for her adoptive mother in her last illness and then brought her father back to live with her. He often spoke appreciatively of her devotion and of his satisfaction in being able to leave her some property. In this case there was some legal complication in the adoption proceedings which had taken place many years previously, and unfortunately she was unable to inherit the money which her parents had not thought of safeguarding by a will.

While death in a family always means a crisis, it does not necessarily mean a broken home in a close-knit, sturdy group, even if the loss is that of a parent. After the first emotional shock has passed, new roles are accepted and the members may draw closer together in a new solidarity if the removal of authority or of financial support is not too complete. Much depends upon the family philosophy and upon traditional ways of meeting difficulties. The personality of the departed may continue to activate the entire group, if kept alive as something dynamic in each member's memory. More than once an adopted child has proved an anchor to sanity and to normal life for a bereft parent who otherwise could hardly face the loneliness and loss.

7

Scientific Aids

While the individual by himself is the subject of physiology and psychology, the family is primarily of sociological concern. Adjustment and readjustment of individuals to differing social situations are peculiarly common to the adoptive family. Such adjusting and interacting are largely the province of the sociologically minded scientist.

The responsibility of parents and of the community for the welfare of children and of old people may be looked upon as an index of the social development of an historic period and of a nation or region within a nation. The oft-enumerated fundamental rights of childhood in the United States include normal home life, opportunities for education, recreation, and vocational preparation for life. They also call for physical, mental, and moral development in harmony with American ideals. Underlying and essential to all the others is the first, namely a home and its family fellowship.

The family represents the smallest group unit of society. It is a little world in itself. It contains most of the elementary problems and some of the complexities that are characteristic of all forms of human association. The adoptive home in all its functions and standards measures up to the biological family in all respects save one: that of customary physical continuation of the race.

Though adoption is about as old as the family itself, it is

only in very recent years that it has reached its full stature as a form of family relationship. From primitive tribal custom to modern oriental and continental European practice, adoption has been tied up with religious beliefs, with inheritance of property, and with exploitation for cheap labor. Only in the modern liberal view of the relationship of parents and children could adoption find a useful place as a social expedient. Its value in this connection is not only to the adoptive parents and children immediately but also in the sense that it improves the future quality of the race by providing nurture to children who would otherwise be neglected. This improvement cannot come, however, unless the nurture is provided by homes of intelligent devotion for children showing reasonable promise of physical, social, and mental competence.

In ancient and even colonial times there were elders who thought in terms of godly parents afflicted with ungodly children, for did not the Bible say: "Children obey your parents in the Lord for this is right." Such authoritarians would stress the first four words but would seldom balance their quotation with another: "Ye fathers, provoke not your children to wrath." Today's view is that the parent wins no rights over his child by what may be incidental, if not unintentional procreation, but he does contract the heaviest responsibilities that man can incur. Obedience, respect, and affection of child for parent are due only in return for such care, discipline, and love as will help the child to the fullest living of his life and as a recognition of the benefits which parents make possible. Such returns are just as fully earned by and freely given to the adoptive as to the natural parent.

With the shift of view from the merely biological to the social, from filial duties to rights and privileges, the way is open for an adoptive relationship equal to that of blood kinship. To find that it surpasses the physical tie in some instances is not surprising when we realize that adoption is undertaken deliberately, usually by people mature of years and of judgment, and that the child often feels a gratitude and an obligation sometimes absent in the average family, though heaven forbid that either family or friends should ever remind the child of indebtedness.

We hear much of the instability of the family of today. We are told that its former functions have been taken away, its ties weakened, its authority and sanctity destroyed. Not without some justice has the home been described as a filling station with a parking space attached. May not the adoptive family have something to offer as an example of stability and social health? The picture is one of parents whose union has survived ten years or more, in itself greater promise of permanence than the early years of haphazard mating; of parenthood voluntarily assumed; of children chosen with some attention to physical and mental and social fitness; and with perhaps an exaggerated mutual need which should tend toward a high type of complementary interaction. This interplay arises largely from the dependency-guardianship qualities inherent in the parent-child relationship and is not necessarily connected with physiological birth.

However satisfactory and permanent the foster relationship may be, adoption is nevertheless an artificial process, hence it needs all possible safeguards for its optimum success. The greatest assurance of its social value is, as has been indicated, a tolerant public opinion. No synthetic relationship will work if it is not socially acceptable. It may safely be said that the soil and climate of the United States, socially speaking, are favorable to adoption. What are some of the most promising checks and aids that science can bring to bear upon it to promote healthy growth?

Perhaps the first scientific contribution is that of the physician whose responsibility it is to determine the bodily fitness of all candidates for the transaction. No home is safe for a child where lurks transmissible disease or disabling weakness. No child is safe as an investment of lifelong labor and affection who bears within him the definite marks of hereditary taint or who has received such unskilled care that his health seems in any danger of permanent impairment. Such unfortunates are sometimes the result of conditions in low-grade maternity homes or baby farms or own home situations. Of course, even a neglected malnourished child can, because of sturdy inheritance, respond astonishingly to highly skilled corrective care. An examination of the child by a pediatrician or a series of examinations if there is any question—including all possible laboratory tests, especially a Wassermann—has come to be one of the first steps in any careful adoption.

A wide variety of physical hazards there are, though some of these science has reduced, hazards that are potential threats to a happy and permanent association. It is no kindness to the physically handicapped or limited child to be adopted except in unusual cases. He will ordinarily be happier and make a better adjustment in an institution for the handicapped or in a boarding home experienced in such care, where he will be free from hopeless competition with physically able children and from the prodding that few parents, own or adoptive, can forbear to give any slow-paced child. The importance of physical examinations for everyone has been so well set forth by public health agencies, by insurance companies, and by other groups that further amplification of this point should not be necessary.

Second only to the need for sound bodies is the necessity of knowing something of mental tendencies and of mental capacities with a view to sustaining lasting ties and carrying out laudable traditions and ambitions. The social and economic status of the family in the community is largely, though not conclusively, the criterion for judgment of the worthiness of the adoptive home, but for the child who is

too young to prove himself and to make choices, some
thought of prevention and prediction must be taken. It is
in this connection that the mental hygienist and psychologist
make their contributions, and because their services are not
generally well known to the layman the remainder of this
chapter will deal briefly with the work of these specialists.

Related to mental capacity yet distinct from it, is mental
health, which is largely the ability to accept life on its own
terms untrammelled by worries and fears, to face reality
with courage and constructive thinking. Any program of
child welfare is likely to have special need of support from
mental hygiene, since the dependent or handicapped child
has been subjected to some strain, possibly to harsh experience which may have left minor scars. The preventive
functioning of mental hygiene will help such scars to heal
permanently. Guidance clinics and mental hygienists have
much to offer the adoptive family or any family that has
behavior problems or maladjustments. It helps as inter-
preter of child to parents and of home to child, and assists
parents and children in their efforts to stand securely and
to pull together.

Child psychology extends beyond traditional and academic limits in its present-day use as a scientific tool in the
solution of such problems as infant training, childhood education, prevention and control of delinquency, diagnosis and
care of the defective and maladjusted, discovery and direction of superior abilities, guidance of parents, foster placement of dependents, and the regulation of adoption. It has
passed from the realm of the theoretical and the experimental to the dependable and the practical. Techniques are
admittedly imperfect but are rapidly improving with their
increased use in schools, in child guidance clinics, in institutions for child care, and in child research centers.

The recent trend has been toward emphasis on the preschool years. It is recognized that the child is a separate

entity, a distinctive personality from the moment of his birth, one with mental and physical potentialities for growth dependent upon his training and surroundings. The protection of the infant's health is widening to include his mental hygiene. Growth is a unifying process. This idea of it is removing undue distinctions between mind and body, between heredity and environment, and between the different scientific disciplines that deal with people.

Dr. Arnold Gesell, one of the leading child psychologists in the United States, and one who has taken a social and active interest in the problems of adoption, believes that the unconscious and subtle effects of child psychology are perhaps more basic for social organization than the obviously humanitarian efforts. He speaks of the infant as a "biological fragment of nature enmeshed in a web of human relationship," and suggests that the interaction between the baby's organic make-up and his social influences is the crucial problem of child development. "For this reason," says he, "the system of child psychology which any culture achieves is an index of that culture. And conversely, the scientific study of the process of mental growth in infant and child becomes a touchstone for the deeper comprehension of the process of social organization itself. Accordingly child psychology belongs at once to the natural and to the social sciences." Is it too much to say that it is a bridge between the two disciplines, over which the feet of children may be led to a finer maturity than humanity has yet achieved?

Present indications point to increasing interest in the social aspects of child psychology. Tests attempt to evaluate not only the child's mental equipment, his "I. Q.," but also his social achievement and potentialities. Habit-training is seen to be not only for the best possible physical and mental well-being but also for pleasanter and more satisfying human relationships. Mental development must not be allowed to outrun social adequacy, and physical growth must keep pace with both. Necessary as social emphasis is for the ordinary child, its importance is many times increased when adoption is involved especially where the child has been exposed to at least two widely different social environments, such as his natural and his foster home, with perhaps an intermediate period in one or more institutions.

Because of the importance of the early years, infancy is in many ways the very best time for adoption. While at no time after social conditioning has begun can he be entirely made over, the child responds more profoundly to foster home influences before school and other outside contacts play upon him. He has had less time to "practice" undesirable responses and reactions. On the other hand there is somewhat greater risk involved in adopting a young child, especially if his antecedents are unknown or unfavorable, *because there is no basis for the belief that native mental inferiority can be overcome by early adoption* or any other treatment. Research has shown, as will be seen in Chapter XII, some improvement in the mental capacity of children adopted into homes superior to those from which they came. Comparatively greater social improvement often results in better adjustment and more capable management of their lives. That is, a really good environment draws out, even stretches out, the inherent potentialities so that a slightly dull child becomes a fairly bright child. "Whatever the environment brings out is hereditary." Nor should it be forgotten that there is a limit to the drawing out. Parents, both natural and adoptive, too often stretch and consequently strain their children beyond their reasonable powers of attainment, not infrequently with disastrous nervous results. If individual improvement is to be at all real, rather than merely apparent, those factors and conditions responsible for betterment—health care, proper clothes, training in manners and speech, widened mental horizons—must be maintained, must be both constant and consistent until "higher" habits are firmly established, until there occurs such ripening of the powers of judgment and insight as belong to experience and maturity.

The psychologist's main contribution to successful adoption, at such an early age that the foster relationships will resemble natural ties, is the developmental diagnosis which will predict not only the child's probable mental capacity but also his *type* of mind, his aptitudes, and his disabilities. The development of infancy is essentially orderly and therefore within the scope of scientific formulation and forecast. Because infant growth is so rapid, the changes undergone from four to six months, from six to nine months, from nine to twelve months are equivalent to the progress which in later childhood it will take years to accomplish. That is, the progress during the early months of life goes by leaps and bounds as compared with later step-by-step development. The characteristics of the infant have a coherent relation to the traits which will emerge in later life. The rate and limits of his growth may also be foreshadowed by the manner and fullness in which he makes the first stages of his journey, say from month to month. Test situations have been devised which bring out characteristic behavior and capacity at each age level. These behavior items are objective and recordable. They relate to motor control, language, adaptive behavior (or intelligence), and personal and social behavior. One test alone is not conclusive at any age level but a series of examinations at stated intervals affords a basis for an objective appraisal, though not for absolute prophecy. We have the motion picture to thank for much of the objectivity in child study. It is possible for placing agencies or for foster parents to expect too much, and they should understand that the aim is not to predict with one hundred per cent accuracy the development of the child, but so to diagnose his case as to reduce the likelihood of error in placement.

The best results may be expected when some of the tests are made after placement and during the probation period, to be compared with those made previous to placement. They may then be interpreted as showing not only the child's developmental history but also the effect of the new family situation upon him. If his capacity increases, it may reasonably be assumed that the home is providing a favorable environment, if other conditions are equally propitious. However, sufficient mental and other examinations should always be made previous to placement to forestall serious mistakes of selection. The dependent child has a right to be spared uprootings and replacements so far as possible, and adopting parents will want to avoid the disappointments of a mistaken selection.

The chosen child, especially the infant, should have at least a year's trial residence with the adopters. This is advisable whether or not the state has such a statutory requirement. A probationary period gives time for impulses and emotions to yield to reason and judgment, gives the child sufficient time to reveal his responses to various stimulations and to the training of the adoptive home, and above all, affords opportunities for a series of unhurried tests to determine his probable abilities and limitations. It should go without saying that such examinations should be done only by competent psychologists. Several different types of predictive tests have been devised but none of them can be automatically given to the child by an unskilled person. Accuracy depends upon expertness and experience, keen observation and careful interpretation. Diagnosis and prognosis, as with the physician, aim to discover *what is* and *what is to be*.

With adequate physical and mental tests given their proper place, and with due attention to heredity where records are available, a child may be taken for adoption with reasonable safety even before his first birthday, if the final decree is withheld for several months to permit family adjustments and final check-ups.

Thus science helps the adoptive family to approximate the biological family, and, other factors being favorable, assures maximum success in the relationship whose goal is permanence in a world where growth is the highest good. Both science and religion would give to every child the opportunity to "increase in wisdom and stature, and in favor with God and man."

PART II

PRIMARILY FOR THOSE WHO SEE
THE ADOPTED CHILD AS A FOCUS
OF PARENTAL AND PROFESSIONAL
RESPONSIBILITY AND WHO WISH
TO EXPLORE THE BROADER FIELD
OF ADOPTION

8

Adoption Folkways

Adoption is probably as old as humanity itself. Among peoples so primitive that the tribe was only an enlarged family, orphans were reared by kinfolk though an infant was sometimes buried with its mother if no woman could be found to nurse it. Two methods of adoption by American Indians were baptism and blood transfusion, after either of which the child was literally considered to be of the same blood as his adopter. Among the Plains Indians of North America, orphans are known to have been adopted by strangers who had lost children, and adoption still plays a part in the clan system of Hopi Indian villages. Relatives often adopt children among the Tewa Indians of New Mexico, about whom an instance is on record of a dying widower who gave his three children to a couple unrelated to him. In the far Pacific on some of the islands of the eastern Torres Straits and Melanesia, babies are adopted before birth and never know who their real parents are. Savages, as well as simpler peoples within our own civilization, commonly have a fondness for children regardless of relationship. For them adoption carries no repugnance whatever; in fact, the orphan child may be treated with exceeding tenderness. Mankind for its own survival must cherish its young.

As humanity advanced from crude beginnings, alliances of the independent tribes were formed and walled cities were built for defense and communal dwelling. This led to freer social exchange and intermarriage between the communities, which broke down tribal barriers and tended toward lessened group responsibilities for such children as lost their parents through the ravages of war and disease. However, three of the ancient nations have left records of provision for orphan children, namely, the Babylonians, the Jews, and the Greeks.

The Babylonians were concerned primarily with protecting the property rights of citizens who had adopted children. Contemporary interest lies mainly in the fact that documentary evidence is provided of the existence of adoption at least four thousand years ago. The Code of Hammurabi, notable among other things because it contains the oldest known laws relating to women and children, provides for the adoption of the illegitimate child and of the child whose living parents give up all claim to him. The adopted child had to be formally acknowledged and could not be cut off from inheritance of property without legal process. If the foster father was an artisan he was bound to teach the adoptive child his trade. Repudiation of the foster parents by the adopted son was severely punished, for instance: "If the son of a palace warder, or of a vowed woman, to the father that brought him up, and to the mother that brought him up, has said, 'Thou art not my father, thou art not my mother,' one shall cut out his tongue." Incidentally it may be of interest to note that Hammurabi reigned in Babylon near the time when, about a thousand miles to the west, Abraham adopted Lot, his brother's son. Hebrew tradition also has it that several hundred years later still, a baby named Moses was picked up adoptively by the daughter of Pharaoh.

The Hebrews gave special care to orphans with something approaching humanitarian motives. In fact, from the days of the Mosaic Law to the present when some of the most forward-looking case work in the United States is being done by Jewish agencies, no people have exceeded the Hebrews in the nurture of dependent children. A spirit of regard for them, implicit in many passages of the Old Testament and the Talmud, was confirmed and reinforced by the teachings of Jesus. Adoption in the modern sense probably did not exist among the ancient Hebrews since in case of childlessness a man could marry another wife to provide heirs. Also to some extent the problem of the care of orphans was solved by the levirate, a custom whereby a brother or other kinsman of the deceased married the widow and fathered the orphans.

Various forms of adoption were to be found in ancient Hebrew times. The barren wife might give a female slave to the husband with a view to adopting the resultant offspring which would be brought forth from the handmaid upon the knees of the adoptive mother. Another adoptive rite was the casting of a garment upon the person to be adopted, such an act implying protection as in the primitive form of marriage where a man spread his garment over a woman. Thus Elijah cast his mantle upon Elisha to indicate that he had adopted Elisha as his spiritual heir. Similarly, Paul speaks of conversion as "adoption" or acceptance as God's children when he says: "Ye have received the spirit of adoption whereby we cry Abba, Father."

With the early Christian church, one solution of the problem was to collect orphans into a large house and pay widows for taking care of them. A little later they were provided for in monasteries, possibly a form of adoption since such children were deemed to belong to the church in a special way.

It should be kept in mind that the two chief reasons for adoption in antiquity were extension of power (*patria potestas*) and provision for continuance of the rites of the family cult. In the patriarchal family of a tribe surrounded by enemies, increase of sons was a condition of survival; concubinage and adoption were acceptable means of continuing male multiplication. Among peoples whose religion or philosophy included ancestor worship, heirs were needed not only to swell the fighting force and for economic reasons but also for sacrificial offerings for the repose of the spirits of the forefathers. In Roman law adoption was practiced only to save a family line from extinction, which limited the number of adopted children per family and prevented the adoption of an only child. In old Hindu and Chinese law, where the religious element predominated, the family system was based not so much on the power of the father as on subordination through affection. A son showed no proper sense of filial duty if he failed to continue his father's line. There was no adoption of girls since succession was provided only through male descendants. The adopted son of old days did not attain the full status of a natural-born son. In Latin he was a "quasi-son," on the same footing as an illegitimate child, with a right to succession but receiving a smaller inheritance; in Sanskrit he was "the reflection of a son."

Present-day Hindu and Chinese laws look upon the adopted son as upon a natural son, and his adoption is sacred and inviolable. In India he has been "invested with the sacred thread" and cannot renounce his status though he may decline his inheritance. In China adoption is dissoluble only for the unfilial conduct of the adopted son.

Thus far there is clearly observable the *family* emphasis rather than the *child* emphasis. This is akin to the general philosophy that sees the individual as existing primarily for the state or the group rather than the state existing primarily for the individual.

Gradually the influence of Christianity, which embodied Jewish ideas and methods as to the care and adoption of children, modified the severity of patriarchal customs and the specific laws of the Roman Empire. Nevertheless,

Roman law still survives as the basis of adoption statutes throughout continental Europe.

Although individual foster care in families was the original idea of the Christian church, at least in the higher levels of civilization, it nearly went out of fashion in the institutional period when monastic orders and sisterhoods established hospitals, homes for the aged, and orphanages. But while adoption was eclipsed by the more spectacular endowed charities, it never went out of existence, and infants deposited at the doors of the churches were taken in by church authorities with a view to their adoption by families.

Meanwhile the problem of dependent children was greatly increased by the European wars. Probably the beginning of the modern period of child welfare work may be marked by the efforts of Saint Vincent de Paul, the religious leader of the seventeenth century who founded the Sisters of Charity and placed in their care great numbers of orphan and homeless children left destitute by the Franco-Austrian war. A revival of individual home care of orphans occurred in the nineteenth century after the Napoleonic decree of 1811 under which the French people boarded out dependent children at national expense. At that time the number of foundlings and abandoned children was enormous, due in part to the Napoleonic wars but more to abuses of privileges offered by the foundling asylums of the time. These were equipped with revolving cribs fixed in the outer walls in such fashion that a child could be placed from the outside and received from the inside, thus shielding the depositor from identification and multiplying unnecessarily the number of children left to public care. The Napoleonic decree provided that newborn foundlings should be placed with a wet-nurse, that crippled and infirm children should be raised in the asylums, and that after the age of six the boarded out children should be placed in country homes whenever possible. After the age of twelve the children were to be apprenticed, the boys to be held in readiness for military service. With some modifications this plan is still in operation in France, the changes being mainly in the direction of greater protection for the adopted child.

In Germany the asylum method has never been so popular as a permanent means of child care as in France and Italy, both of whose child welfare practices have been closely parallel. While Germany has had the largest orphanages in the world, that country has, nevertheless, systematically placed dependent children in families. The custom has been to place the child temporarily in an institution until a suitable home could be found. Both the public authorities and the religious groups have followed this practice. Adoption has increased since the World War to such an extent that a National Adoption Office has been established in Leipzig, which works in co-operation with local adoption bureaus. Two possible reasons for this increase are the growing number of childless marriages and the fact that the prejudice against illegitimate children is vanishing. The rate of illegitimacy is very high in Germany and such children furnish a large proportion of the candidates for adoption.

Under feudalism which was the prevailing social and economic system for centuries in Europe, every man owed loyalty and service in peace and in war to his overlord, and in return he received protection and the means of support. Children were considered tributary to the welfare of the manor and hence when they became dependent they had a recognized right to support within the economic group. If the particular manor failed to discharge its duty toward an orphan, church charity usually supplied the lack.

In England when feudalism began to disintegrate late in the fourteenth century, the number of destitute persons left stranded by the passing of the manorial system increased greatly. These wandering beggars uprooted from feudal estates and without means of support or protection, were finally deprived of the last crumbs of comfort by the impoverishment of the Roman Catholic·Church whose monasteries and lands had been seized by Henry VIII. When Elizabeth came to the throne she was faced by vast numbers of subjects in the extremity of misery, and in 1601 the first act was passed that recognized the right of paupers to support from public taxes. This statute allowed each community, now called a parish instead of a manor, to tax itself for the care of destitute children. The older ones could be given work to do, or they could be apprenticed. Those who were too young to work were "farmed out" or put in poorhouses along with adult indigents.

In both England and America the system of indenture was important as a means of caring for dependent children and was a step toward adoption, even when it did not directly have that result. Under the guilds, indenture had been purely a business contract whereby parents apprenticed a child to a craftsman to learn his trade. Indenture was never well suited to the care of young children and led to abuses of which Charles Dickens only touched the fringe. After the Industrial Revolution overseers of the poor trafficked in pauper children with millowners; apprenticeship became slavery with wages denied; decent food and clothes the exception; six- to eight-year-olds collapsed in their tasks only to be quickly replaced by new recruits—such was the picture! Yet indenture was probably better than herding together in the mixed almshouses young children with the insane, the criminal, the sick, the aged, and the generally derelict; for apprenticeship gave, at least theoretically, to each child an individual or a family who was responsible for his support and care in an environment quantitatively less dangerous. In some measure indenture supplanted the outgrown idea of feudalism. The individual could now be more firmly planted in a given locality with a fixed social status. "Binding out" thus tied the homeless child to a family and a community and especially in the American colonies it often led to virtual, if not legal, adoption.

The orphan asylum in Britain and America may be considered another move forward in child welfare, though one that had too much of militaristic strictness in it and was quite out of step with enlightened modern thinking and practice. The orphan asylum, founded by religious and philanthropic groups, did succeed measurably in sifting out the children from the mixed almshouse population. These privately supported and controlled asylums were subject to public inspection. They made some efforts toward the education of inmates, though such training did little more than point to domestic service. Gradually it dawned on the public mind that by making a small investment in a dependent child, instead of providing only the most meagre care, he might be taken out of the pauper class and made into an efficient adult worker. To this end the large institution gave way to small grouped homes or scattered ones, and to boarding out, especially of infants, which always leads to a certain amount of adoption.

The nineteenth century saw the development of differentiated treatment of children in public care, first the segregation of deaf, crippled, blind, and feebleminded children in certified institutions where they received special care and training, and late in the century the emigration of selected boys and girls especially in England. Altogether, the eighteenth and nineteenth centuries, with their rising industrial values and falling human estimates afford some very black pages in the history of child welfare. Yet the discerning eye can see that the trend was upward, and that the foundations of more scientific treatment were being laid.

The beginnings of selective placement in England can be traced in the Barnardo Homes of London which combined institutional and foster home care. From 1866 to 1915 Dr. Thomas Barnardo rescued 82,126 homeless children, placed them in institutions, and wherever possible later returned them to their rehabilitated homes. The majority, however, were placed in foster families, first in England, later in Canada and other British colonies, and a large number of these were adopted. Up to 1918 the Barnardo Homes had sent 26,281 child emigrants overseas.

Two British societies, organized for the purpose of arranging adoptions, date from the period of the World War. The National Children Adoption Association was started to help care for Belgian babies but its work was soon extended to include native infants. This agency places illegitimate children almost exclusively, as does the National Adoption Society founded before the World War, in Cambridge, but it was very limited in scope until 1919 when it became established in London with the object of providing homes for war orphans or those legally fatherless.

England did not legalize adoption until 1926, although it had been unofficially practiced somewhat on a *de facto* basis. The English Adoption Act embodies the modern motive of conferring "the privileges of parents upon the childless and the protection of parents upon the parentless." This idea keeps uppermost the well-being of the child as opposed to the former notion of strengthening the family. Some critics maintain that certain revisions are desirable, chiefly in the direction of procuring for the adopted child the rights of succession and inheritance, for adoption does not include property rights in England though a will may be made in favor of the adopted child. However, the law on the whole seems to be working out satisfactorily. It has resulted in a great increase in the number of adoptions and in a considerable saving to the taxpayers. Many adoptive parents have expressed themselves as happy in the foster relationship and as feeling secure in the legal sanction which gives them undisputed claim to their child.

It is the observation of officers of the courts that the children adopted "appear to be getting much better homes than the large majority of the children in the homes of the working classes where there are a number of children." The National Adoption Society reports an increasing number of applicants for a second child. That the legal and social wheels do not yet turn with perfect smoothness is shown by the appointment, a decade after the Adoption Act of 1926, of a special Committee on Adoption Societies and Agencies to inquire into the "evils associated with unlicensed, unregulated and unsupervised adoption" and into "the methods pursued by adoption societies." Some of the "evils" found were lack of sufficient social investigation, omission of medical examinations, lack of uniformity in probation policy. Adoption societies were found to be receiving payments from mothers, putative fathers and adopters, with some actual sale of babies by doctors and midwives. Recommendations included compulsory medical and social examination of children and of adopters; a three-month probation period; licensing and supervision of adoption societies; prohibition of advertisements offering or seeking children for adoption.

In 1930 Scotland brought forth its own Adoption of Children Act modelled on the English act but with some differences in practice due to the fact that the customary method of care for dependent children has been to board them out with widows or married couples, in contrast to that of England where institutional care has predominated. Secrecy is the main feature of the proceedings and reports do not disclose names. The welfare of the child is the primary object.

The American development of systematized child-placing began in the middle of the nineteenth century with the founding of the Children's Aid Society of New York. Its original purpose was to send destitute city children to distant country homes, though it differed from the British plan by largely omitting the preliminary institutional care. While this was not technically indenture, the system of emigration was not entirely free from its evils, since service by the child was an essential feature. In addition to placing children singly in foster homes, as applications were received, large groups of children were sent out in the care of an agent to a central location where applicants could inspect and choose, after the manner of a cattle fair, except that no price was demanded. Such parties were also sent out on tours for the purpose of gaining money and publicity for the supporting institution. From New York and New England, up and down the Atlantic seaboard, these children went, singing and serving as an exhibit while an agent described the work and made a plea for funds.

The first state children's home society was founded in Illinois and was followed by thirty or more similar state societies, so-called because they were state-wide in scope and activities though not administered by the government. These societies placed children in free family homes and legal adoption frequently followed. Eventually these agencies affiliated under the name of the National Children's Home Society which later became the National Children's Home and Welfare Association. Some of this organization's professional activities have been connected with the National Conference of Social Work and the Child Welfare League of America.

The Charity Organization Society with its beginnings in Buffalo and in Boston in 1877 and 1879, respectively, emphasized case work. An appeal of this period for family homes of varying kinds read in part:

The Boston Children's Aid Society wishes to find homes in the city, suburbs or country, where poor children who are homeless, destitute, or exposed, may enjoy a happy and wholesome family life, instead of being subject to the exposure of the streets, or the crowded, artificial life of institutions. Kind care, good example, moral training, real friends, everything in fact that a welcome in a good home implies—that is what we wish to secure for our boys

and girls. We urge you to consider whether your own doors may
not be thrown open to rescue, relieve, and protect some unfortunate child, and whether you can tell us of other families with
whom these children may perhaps find a welcome.

The types of homes specified were, first of all those "homes
in which children of any age may be adopted." There were
also free temporary homes, working or wage homes for older
children, working or wage homes for mothers with a small
child, boarding homes, and emergency or temporary homes.
To the case worker of the 1930's this may seem a somewhat
naïve method of home finding but it deserves the respect
that should be accorded to all trail blazers.

From such small beginnings grew a national pattern of
child welfare work with placing out predominant and adoption as a widespread practice. The early efforts at child-
placing were individualistic and well-meaning based on immediate relief of distress, but with little in the way of a comprehensive program. Community responsibility for the welfare of all children is the present ideal of service, one phase
of which is the provision of homes for the homeless.

For many years the success of a state children's home society, or similar organization, was measured by the number
of children received and placed in homes, but of late the
criteria have been qualitative rather than quantitative.
Many of the societies are now placing a smaller number of
children than formerly, due to constructive efforts of the
trained social worker toward preserving the child's own
home and to more careful selection of the children for adoption; also because of the trend toward publicly supported
state agencies.

More than one half the states have agencies with authority
to place children in family homes and in many states there
are county agencies with such authority. Most of the metropolitan centers have municipal agencies. There are still

other societies, none of them public, that cut across county or state lines and give service on a regional basis, such as the New England Home for Little Wanderers. Nearly all institutions for dependent children eventually place out a large proportion of their children, since few are equipped to care for their charges until they reach the age and condition of self-support, and because they recognize the disadvantage of too long a period of institutional care.

Among privately supported placement agencies are those of the Catholic, Jewish, and numerous Protestant denominations as well as many nondenominational and fraternal bodies. The American Legion has a differentiated national program for the care of children of ex-service men.

The White House Conference of 1909 called by President Theodore Roosevelt was one of the beacons pointing toward the co-ordination and integration of work for dependent children. Two hundred strong, the leaders came from every state in the union. These people represented state boards of charity, children's aid associations, children's home societies, societies for the prevention of cruelty to children, orphan asylums, juvenile reformatories, and the various religious bodies, as well as people of no religious affiliation. In spite of the size and diversity of the gathering, it adopted by unanimous vote a platform of child helping. A few of its conclusions with reference to homeless children were these:

Home life is the highest and finest product of civilization. It is the great molding force of mind and character. . . .

As to children who for sufficient reasons must be removed from their own homes, or who have no homes, it is desirable that, if normal in mind and body and not requiring special training, they should be cared for in families wherever practicable. The carefully selected foster home is for the normal child the best substitute for the natural home. Such homes should be selected by a most careful process of investigation, carried on by skilled agents through personal investigation and with due regard to the religious faith of the child. After children are placed in homes, adequate visitation—with careful consideration of the physical, mental, moral, and spiritual training and development of each child on the part of the responsible home-finding agency—is essential. . . .

An important result of the conference was the creation of the Children's Bureau, acclaimed the first public agency in the world whose function was to consider as a whole the condition, problems, and welfare of childhood. A legislative act, passed in 1912, authorized the establishment of the bureau, which was directed to "investigate and report . . . upon all matters pertaining to the welfare of children and child life among all classes of our people."

In 1919 at the request of President Wilson, the Children's Bureau called a second conference of representatives of child welfare work throughout the United States. Committees appointed to formulate minimum standards for the protection of children in need of special care reaffirmed the conclusions of the first White House Conference and adopted additional resolutions with reference to examination before placement of the child's "health, mentality, character, and family history and circumstances." The importance of records was emphasized, both those having to do with the child's background and with his development while under agency care.

Again, during President Hoover's administration in 1930, a third White House Conference on Child Health and Protection considered the needs of the nation's children and emphasized, as previous conferences had done, the importance of keeping families together where possible. This conference reiterated the need for scientific placement in foster homes especially when adoption is a likely outcome. Almsgiving or philanthropy as a way of caring for the homeless child is definitely and increasingly on the wane. Proper care is his birthright and this is the responsibility of the community and the nation—such is the marked trend in belief and practice today.

Another shift in emphasis has to do with seeing the whole child in perspective and in relation to his social setting: health, education, leisure, home, labor, and special abilities or handicaps. The ambitious program of this 1930 conference, as stated by President Hoover, was "to study the present status of the health and well-being of the children of the United States . . . ; to report what is being done; to recommend what ought to be done and how to do it." The machinery set up to accomplish the task consisted of 1,200 committee members working for a year on nation-wide studies of children and of the forces affecting their development. The tangible results of the work were the Children's Charter and several volumes of committee findings and recommendations. All this indicates the tendency to see wholes and interrelations in the treatment of special fields.

A milestone in child protection was reached when the Children's Bureau was founded. Its services have consisted of research, such as collection and analysis of facts about children, gathered by first-hand investigation or library study, reporting of discovered facts, co-operation with states and with public and private organizations. It has helped to integrate the varied child welfare programs throughout the country, to raise their standards, and to give them dignity and prestige. It has put the dependent child in his proper place, not as something peculiar and set apart, but as one of many problems arising inevitably out of present social conditions to be solved with all the skill and consideration that can be brought to bear. The subjects in which the Children's Bureau is especially interested are those having to do with health, social welfare, and employment. Studies have been made concerning the physical growth and care of the child, prenatal to maturity, and bulletins are issued for parents as well as in the fields of medicine, nursing, and public health. The early years of the bureau were concerned primarily with life and health: birth registrations, maternal and infant mortality, and diseases of children. More recently the emphasis has shifted to social welfare: child labor, dependency, delinquency, education, and recreation.

A feature of the work of the bureau since 1935 has been the administration of funds appropriated under the Social Security Act for co-operation "with State public welfare departments in establishing, extending and strengthening . . . public services for the protection and care of homeless, dependent, and neglected children." Another growing function is consultation service, as national, state, and regional agencies in professional, civic, labor, and other fields turn to the bureau for advice. Co-operation extends not only to organizations within our own country, but to international bodies such as the League of Nations and various Pan-American alliances.

One of the most recent Children's Bureau ventures is a study of foster home placement and adoption. There is in progress (1939) an analysis of all legislation for the protection of children under care away from their own homes, including an examination of problems in about two thousand adoption cases and evaluation of the services and procedures of state departments which have made social investigations in connection with petitions for adoption.

Another agency of national scope that has done much to stimulate interest in adoption as well as to improve procedure, is the Child Welfare League of America, organized in 1920. It grew out of a "Bureau for the Exchange of Information," a clearing house for child-placing agencies, particularly to facilitate the care and supervision of placed out children whose foster parents moved from one state to another. Its membership consists of some one hundred and fifty constituent organizations such as children's aid societies, state and county agencies, and institutions which place children in family homes. Its purpose is to improve organized service for physically, mentally, and socially handicapped children in the United States and Canada, through consultation, study of community or other programs, regional conferences, and interchange of service. It has been of special helpfulness during the depression by its insistence on the dangers of mass consideration, and on the appraisal of remedial measures on the basis of their accord with sound principles of child care regardless of stress and emergency. The league is at present (1939) engaged on a nation-wide investigation of adoption practices with the aim of co-ordinating the laws of the different states, of preventing the bootlegging of babies, of increasing protective measures, of putting out of business extralegal maternity homes and baby farms, of enforcing a probation period. This program and that of the Children's Bureau parallel surprisingly the 1937 report of the English Committee on Adoption Societies and Agencies mentioned earlier in the chapter.

It is impossible to estimate accurately the extent of adoption in the United States because separate records are not usually kept by the courts to show how many petitions are approved. Such records as there are may be difficult to consult owing to their confidential nature. Information available for several metropolitan regions and for states where the law requires investigation of all petitions shows an adoption rate of about thirty per 100,000 population. Recent figures by the Children's Bureau indicate a higher rate for urban areas, ranging up to one hundred adopted children per 100,000 population. However, it is unsafe to use these figures as a basis for a country-wide calculation of a practice in which there is so much local variation. More detailed estimates are given in Chapter IX.

The forward march of scientific procedure stands in some danger of at least a temporary halt due to curtailment of funds. Not only have public and private agencies suffered greatly in the depression years (1930–1940) but also the training of workers and the pursuit of research projects have been slowed up. On the other hand there continues a lively, determined spirit of fact finding and fact facing in both national and state government. When child welfare proponents embark upon a program of statutory reform whereby it is aimed to reconcile divergent stateways with modern enlightened folkways, the outlook for childhood is promising.

The all-inclusive folkway of mankind has been its generalized regard for the young of the species. The course of human survival has ever depended upon the care of children. Any civilization in its own day, and as tested by historic time, can be measured in terms of high or low degree by the way it has treated its children.

9

Social Work Foundations

As the preceding chapters have pointed out, adoption is primarily a sociological problem of human relationships. The techniques for handling the problem are mainly furnished by social work and by the law, both indispensable and almost inextricably bound together in today's practices.

Since the World War the care of dependent children has been of increasing concern to all civilized countries, and the last decade has shown world-wide advance in public opinion, in legislation, and in social work. Some of these forward steps have been taken under the guidance of the League of Nations whose humanitarian projects are significant for child welfare. Information and co-operation were quickly forthcoming, not only from member nations but from peoples who had hitherto not been sympathetic to the objectives of the league. It is a commentary on world unrest that delegates have reported an increase of abandoned and cruelly treated children in various countries, tragic first-fruits of the insecurity and strained nerves of their elders. A unique document in the annals of child welfare is the Declaration of Geneva in 1925:

1. The child must be given the means requisite for its normal development both materially and spiritually.
2. The hungry child must be fed, the sick child nursed, the backward child helped, the delinquent child reclaimed, the orphan and the waif succored and sheltered.

3. In all times of distress the child must be the first to receive relief.
4. The child must be placed in a position to earn a livelihood and must be given protection against every form of exploitation.
5. The child must be brought up in the consciousness that its talent should be devoted to the service of its fellowmen.

The Commission for Protection and Welfare of Children and Young People, one of the five permanent advisory commissions of the League, has made a study of legislation and types of service for child protection in different lands. By making available its findings the Child Welfare Committee has brought about a cross-fertilization of ideas of widespread influence. In the ten-year period of this inquiry measures of protection have been provided in country after country, many of them incorporating principles of child-caring borrowed from other nations. A subcommittee of the league, formed in 1935 to study child placement, reported in 1938 the status of foster home care in twenty-six countries representing every continent.

World thinking on the subject of placement seems to be that institutional and family care are supplementary; that family care is advantageous for the homeless child without blood ties; that adoption under proper safeguards is the most satisfactory type of foster care for the child bereft of parental guardianship. Unfortunately the reports so far have not differentiated adoption from other forms of foster family care in many countries so that few comparisons can be made. It is plain that while adoption is legally provided for in nearly all civilized nations, the number of children adopted is small compared with those in other foster homes and in institutions, though rapidly increasing in Great Britain, France, and Germany. Selective placement by case work methods is most highly specialized in the United States and Canada. However, training is being developed for placement workers on both a professional and volunteer basis in some of the European countries.

In the United States there is little more unity of program for child welfare than there is likeness of climate or topography. Not only are there forty-eight systems of administration and function, but also in various cities there are many differences of standards, methods, and emphases, more or less independent of the states in which they happen to be. Some of the extremes of foster care range from that in North Carolina with 94 per cent of its dependent children in institutions, to Massachusetts with only 23 per cent institutionalized. Public support is the rule for over half the total number in Massachusetts, Minnesota, and Ohio, both in public institutions and in boarding foster homes. In contrast, 99 per cent of the dependent children of Louisiana are cared for under private responsibility, mainly in church-supported institutions. Some cities, notably Cincinnati, Chicago, Indianapolis, and New York, provide for many children at public expense in the care of private agencies. Organizations supported by church or fraternal groups give service on a local, a regional, or a national basis. A socially alert community provides for its destitute children through such means as a children's aid society, a "children's bureau," children's institutions, a protective society, or a family welfare agency. Probably in no field of social work is there greater diversity of standards, of motivation, or of concept of the task than in child welfare.

Present day methods of child-caring in the United States and Canada are colored by a mixed legal heritage; common law survivals along the Atlantic seaboard, civil law principles reflected on the Pacific coast, in the Gulf States, and in French Canada, blurred and modified, yet still discernible reminders of earlier days.

A characteristic of Canadian child welfare work is the partnership of state and citizen exemplified in the children's aid societies found in eight of the nine provinces. All honor to the Child Welfare League of America in its efforts to co-ordinate the laws and practices of the two countries, so alike in background and so closely linked by their transcontinental frontier. A unified policy is needed for border states and provinces as much as for different states, as is indicated by several puzzling cases that have been brought before the courts.

It is difficult not to be impatient with the restrictions and delays arising out of state differences of administration and legislation. Children's needs are so urgent and change so rapidly that often an opportunity postponed is one forever lost for that particular child. This is especially true in adoption for if placement has to be long delayed in order to clear up legal tangles or to determine agency responsibility, the child may cease to be adoptable. Not only do most adopters prefer a small child as being more like their own, but a long period in an institution or in a series of temporary boarding homes may unfit a child for the emotional interplay of family life. Yet the most skillful social worker and her legal advisor sometimes stand helpless before the tightly knotted involvements of interstate child welfare problems.

To attempt to hold in mind a composite picture of social work in relation to adoption is as difficult as trying to see all the details of a Flemish painting at a glance. The foregoing paragraphs highlight in quick succession only a few of the varied approaches.

Regardless of administrative differences in America, case work is the unifying methodological factor in handling adoptions. Aided by individualized social service the adoptive family can reach its full possibilities, not only of satisfaction to itself but of value to the race as a stable and productive unit.

The first step in the child-family situation is to make certain that the child cannot possibly be cared for by his own people. Often a study of the case reveals the difficulty to be temporary. The family may be kept together if it is given financial aid in a crisis, or if the children can be boarded out for a few weeks while the parent recovers from an illness. Again, the child who does not have competent parents may yet have other relatives who can and should care for him, possibly with a little help. When it has been ascertained that there is no hope of the child's finding a permanent home with his own kin, he is scrutinized carefully to make sure that he has no defects of physical or mental nature that will bar him from adoption, and this decision often cannot be made offhand. He may require a period of residence in an institution or in a boarding home to eliminate bad habits, to build up his health, or to be given sufficient tests and observation to establish his personality type and capacity. All this requires the most sympathetic handling of both the child and his own relatives.

The home-finder's task includes an investigation of the heredity of the prospective adopters; their material resources; their intellectual, cultural, and religious levels; and the personality make-up of all members of the foster family. The fine art of case work is achieved when the placement is mutually stimulating and satisfying to both child and parents. The overgrown, good-natured boy, strong but clumsy, used to hardship and in need of plenty of elbow room, may in a city home track mud into the house, break the best china, and spoil his clothes; and eventually become so discouraged as to make a poor school record. The same child might thrive on a farm where he would have responsibility and physical exercise in the care of cows, pigs, and chickens.

Before the days of preplacement investigation, a musically gifted girl was placed in a home where music was considered "unprofitable" if not sinful. Although she received good physical care and affection she became morose and disobedient and was returned to the agency as a failure. This time some "personality diagnosis" was made before she was again placed in a family where both father and mother were musical. Here she blossomed into a happy, ambitious, and appreciated daughter.

These are examples of obvious placement problems. Often the factors are more subtle, occasionally requiring the services of a psychiatrist to disentangle, or, where there are no pathological elements, mental hygiene and psychology may furnish the needed guidance.

The home-finder, then, tries to see the situation as a whole; she looks upon the child not only as an organism but also as a person with a history and with certain potentialities. The home must be considered as to its possibilities and attitudes, and must be evaluated in its community setting. It is absolutely essential that both home and child be viewed as to the probable effect of the one upon the other. This is sometimes difficult because the adopting parents are under unusual emotional strain and may behave quite unlike themselves.

Nor is the case finished when the pieces in the social puzzle are finally fitted together and the adopting household is open to the homeless child. There remains the probation period during which the supervisor's task is mainly that of interpretation of child to parents, of parents to child, perhaps of neighborhood and child to each other, with whatever guidance may be needed in parental responsibility. Only when the adoption decree is granted are the social worker's services discontinued, and even then the case records must be guarded against the time when parents or child may want the very information refused at the time of placement.

It occasionally happens that for some reason legal adoption is not feasible even though there exists a strong tie between a child and a foster family. A solution for such ambiguity may lie in guardianship which affords most of the privileges without the full responsibilities of adoption.

It is not a substitute for adoption because it offers less security for the child, but it is occasionally practicable in unusual situations. Guardianship is of two kinds, either for protection of property or of person. Corporate guardianship with custody in the states which allow it may provide a satisfactory way out of certain difficulties.

A case in point is that of a small problem boy who was placed out by an agency in a superior boarding home. After nine years of almost unbelievable improvement on the part of the child and of strong mutual attachment between him and his foster mother, a single woman, she was obliged to move to another state. Adoption was out of the question due to legal complications, and separation was a painful thought to both. A satisfactory solution was reached when the foster mother took personal guardianship of the child in the state in which she was establishing residence.

Adoption is the legal substitute for the true parent-child relationship, and should be entered into for no other reason. Where the connection is not intended to be permanent or complete, some other arrangement such as guardianship is preferable. In cases where the inheritance of property is the main consideration, a will may be all that is necessary.

The extent of adoption in the United States is problematical, largely because of state and regional differences in record-keeping and in attitude toward adoption as a social expedient. It was estimated in 1934 by J. Prentice Murphy, long identified with children's work on a nation-wide scale, that there were 400,000 dependent children being cared for by 2,000 agencies throughout the country. Reports from Minnesota, Illinois, Pennsylvania, and Massachusetts between 1924 and 1932 agreed on approximately the same rate of adoption, about thirty per 100,000 population. However, this is not necessarily a safe estimate for the entire country, as we have already indicated. The 1933 census of Dependent and Neglected Children indicates that the distribution of children in all foster homes was proportionately highest in the New England, Middle Atlantic, and East North Central states, and lowest in the South Atlantic, East South Central, and West South Central groups. During 1933 the number of legal adoptions reported was 5,833 or 4.9 per cent of the 119,646 dependent children discharged from agencies and institutions during 1933. In thirty-five states over one half of such children were in institutions. Those in free or boarding foster homes that were on probation or that would eventually be adopted, cannot be estimated.

The ages of all children receiving care either in institutions or foster homes ranged from infancy to twenty years, with considerably over one half of them between six and thirteen years of age, and relatively few under one year. Again, there is no basis for more than a guess at the number of adoptable children in the different age groups. It must be emphasized that only a very rough estimate of adoption can be reached. Reports do not differentiate adoption sufficiently from other foster home care, and much adopting still goes on without the intervention of any recognized agency or organization, regrettable and hazardous as this may be. Also, court records frequently do not separate adoption decrees from other business.

The trend is toward less institutional and less free foster home care for dependent children, except for that in adoptive homes; in this last, the trend seems to be increasing. Some social workers estimate that adoptions will soon decrease due to more careful case work and higher standards for adoptive homes. Moreover, the supply of small children seems destined to diminish in view of the fact that present figures indicate a rather rapidly aging general population.

A puzzling question to the layman in child welfare work is the distinction between the public and private agency. Indeed this perplexes social workers themselves when private philanthropic funds are curtailed by income taxes and other means and when public agencies are swamped by Social Security administration and abnormal relief loads. In normal times it is the task of the private agency, with a smaller case load, to do more experimental work, more interpreting to the public, and perhaps to give more time to influencing legislation or the courts. Many of the rather standardized techniques of the public institution have been taken over from the approved experimental methods of the private organizations. Both have their place and more or less complement each other. Some states pay a private agency to do a certain type of work, instead of duplicating through their own organizations. Whether the private or the public agency will offer the better service in a given situation is almost as personal a matter as the choice of a physician. The private agency is usually more flexible and so may be better equipped to handle an exceptional case. On the other hand, to certain people the anonymity of a big impersonal institution may be more appealing. No rules can be laid down, except to caution adopters and all others who contemplate dealings with a private agency to make sure that it is licensed and approved by the state and that it is qualified by a high type of professionally trained workers to give adequate service. Most states consider their duty done when they license suitable agencies and make little attempt to keep out of business the commercial or sentimental bureau that purports to give child welfare services. The public can quickly make such ventures unprofitable by refusing to patronize them.

There is need for a more enlightened public opinion regarding child welfare aids. Wisconsin, with its fine Children's Code, found that administration was lagging behind the statutes, largely for lack of general information. It attributes a rather radical change of attitude toward adoption to an educational campaign sponsored jointly by public and private groups. Many of the tragedies of haste and concealment would be avoided if there were a more general appreciation of social services, if it were understood that good case work means neither glaring publicity nor undue coercion. Even some public officials and professional men need to be informed of the value of protective social devices, so that they may not think it necessary to wink at the law to "protect" a client or a prominent family.

Illinois, as late as 1937, in its child welfare laws provided neither for preliminary investigation nor for the subsequent trial period in connection with adoption. This lack in child welfare provisions, inconsistent with its general advance in social welfare, encourages practices with regard to child-placing that are disapproved by the best social work authorities elsewhere in the country. For more than a decade efforts have been made by social workers to correct the more serious defects but progressive proposals have been resisted.

Social work and law agree today, as regards adoption, in placing the emphasis on the child. Parents, natural and adoptive, have their claim but that of the child is prior and if a conflict occurs his welfare will be the determining factor. Lawyers, judges, and social workers act together, ideally at least, to free the child from restrictions imposed by conflicting laws, by negative interpretations, or by institutional rules made to avoid expense or to win credit. A lawyer suggests that one value of the work of social agencies lies in the filling of gaps left by the adoption statutes, though he fears that welfare organizations sometimes defeat their own ends by excessive red tape, so that adopters and natural parents become impatient and resort to advertising and other hazardous short cuts. Perhaps that is because the general public has not yet reached the place where it puts the rights of children above its own selfish wishes.

This chapter has touched upon some of the child welfare or social work aspects of adoption: scope, extent, trends, administration, and methodology. Now we come to a consideration of the legal and judicial phases, the tough cement that holds together the disconnected fragments of the various contributing disciplines and builds a firm wall of security about the adopted child.

10

Legal Foundations

In common law there was no sanction for adoption but it was an old custom under the civil law. Adoption statutes began to appear in this country by the middle of the nineteenth century. The early statutes prescribed a process by which the custody of a child could be transferred or an heir provided by deed, by special legislative act, or by contract. Today all the states and territories of the United States, as well as the District of Columbia, have adoption statutes which require court procedure. Most of them have either enacted new legislation or made important amendments in the last fifteen years, with a trend toward greater administrative and court supervision of adoption. There has also been a considerable amount of legislation in related fields, as the licensing and supervision of placing agencies, maternity homes, and hospitals; the prohibition of advertising for or of children to adopt; the extension of the adopted child's rights to include such benefits as Workmen's Compensation and Mother's Aid. Recent legislation reflects a growing emphasis on the human elements involved in adoption, particularly on the individual needs of the child. This is shown in provisions for consent by the natural parents, guardian, or other specified person; in the requirements for pre-adoption investigation; in an enforced and supervised period of trial residence in the adoptive home; and in provisions for preservation of records.

While these protective features of adoption legislation are directed mainly toward the child as the most helpless and easily exploited person involved, in many states the welfare of natural parents and adopters is guarded, often against their own impulsiveness and unwisdom. Most states that provide for an investigation require a report as to why the natural parents, if living, are willing or obliged to give up the child. This, together with the almost unanimous requirement of relinquishment or consent to the adoption by the parents or other close kindred if they can be found, is a check for the too ready breaking of ties or abandonment of obligations. The investigation also includes an inquiry into the financial and moral ability of the petitioners to bring up and educate the child, and in some instances, into their religious affiliation in order to ascertain that the child will be reared in the faith of his parents. Another common requirement of the investigation is an examination of the "physical and mental health of the child" to determine his adoptability and his fitness for the proposed home.

About one half of the states have statutory provision for some sort of pre-adoption investigation, and in one fourth of the states the state department of public welfare is authorized to arrange investigations. In a few states investigation is in the hands of a local agency; in other states the court arranges for it either through one of its own officers or through a local agency. Several points in favor of making the state welfare department responsible are that it insures state-wide uniformity of adoption practice; it may be more effective before the courts; it is more likely to be impartial; it provides a centralized and guarded repository for records. When county departments or other local agencies, public or private, have adequate facilities they may be called on by the state department of public welfare. In some states where a welfare department makes the investigation it merely reports to the court; in others it makes a recommendation regarding the desirability of the adoption. Experience is proving the inadequacy of the thirty-day limit for investigation that some statutes impose.

Whatever the administrative method and details—and the matter is still in the experimental stage in many states that have taken steps in preplacement inquiry—the importance of some sort of impartial social investigation can hardly be overestimated. While informed individual adopters can safeguard themselves in their choice of a child, it is only by fairly uniform provisions for investigation by a responsible and socially competent authority that adoption can safely be utilized to its full possibility as a means of child nurture.

Not only is wise legislation needed but it must have the backing of public opinion. The first step may well be the building up of enlightened sentiment that demands, or at least endorses, the desirable changes.

One state with careful provisions on its statutes for investigation found that they were not being carried out in certain counties. A check-up disclosed that "laws (affecting children) may never be read by the very individuals entrusted by ballot and by appointment with the duties of administration." A department of the state government was, therefore, asked to undertake a campaign of adult education about measures of protection for children, which lifted the level of thinking and practice perceptibly. A program of this sort can be carried out through organized groups such as bar associations, medical associations, parent-teacher associations, service clubs, and other civic and professional groups. In a reasonable time such constructive effort can do much to raise a state or region from a "social frontier" to an enlightened community where judges, lawyers, doctors, ministers, and social workers co-operate in law enforcement and legislative reform, and where leading citizens themselves become adoptive parents.

Another necessity for the implementing of laws concerning investigation is the provision of funds and case workers. An already overburdened and underfinanced agency cannot in a moment enter upon large-scale home-finding merely by the magic of an amendment or a flawless new code. Those interested in improving adoption statutes would do well to study local conditions and attitudes to make sure the proposed legislation suits existing needs and machinery.

The laws of about one third of the states require that the child shall live in the home of the petitioner for at least six months before the final decree is granted. The trial period is one year in a few other states, in some of which the court makes an interlocutory decree, and requires supervisory visits by a representative of the welfare department or by the court. Supervision may be unnecessary or undesirable when the placement has been made by a qualified agency or when the child is a relative, though even in such cases the new relationship may sometimes be greatly strengthened by an objective minded supervisor. In non-agency placements supervision is almost unquestionably needed. Perhaps the safest device to meet this problem is a provision for supervision with authority for waiver given to the welfare department.

In many states the trial period may be waived or reduced by the court. The trial residence is not only a safeguard against impulsive decisions by the petitioner or natural relatives or against insufficient investigation, but, more important, it also affords time for social adjustment within the adoptive family. Not all types of personality can be fitted together comfortably under one roof, and no measurement yet devised can take the place of day by day living together. Thus the waiver appears to be an unfortunate weakening of a valuable device. In one state that has a six-months residence requirement a decree was recently made when the child was three days old, in accordance with plans made before his birth. It is not easy to see the advantage of such haste in taking the final and irrevocable step. After six months or a year the adopters would have been able to determine with far more accuracy whether or not the baby was desirable, physically and mentally sound, and whether or not their household was suited to the demands of such a young child.

Since adoption is wholly statutory, recent enactments generally supersede former methods and must be strictly followed, as is shown by the decisions of sixty-eight cases in twenty-seven states since 1925. Courts have held that adoptions by deed or other outmoded process were invalid if completed after the enactment requiring court procedure.[1]

Occasionally an old law may be dug up whose jagged bones serve to cut "red tape." That children can still be deeded, even in a state with constructive provisions, is indicated by the following news item appearing in a city newspaper dated February 22, 1939: "Man 'Deeds' Son to Couple 'For $10 and Other Considerations.' . . . When it became apparent that endless difficulties lay in the way of adopting the boy through the regular channels, because of the inability to locate the mother and obtain her consent and signature, . . . the lawyer resorted to the 'deed' method, relying on an old statute which appears to provide authority for such action." Would this disposition hold, if contested?

As shown by the tables in the next chapter all the jurisdictions of the United States now require some form of court procedure. There are many differences of detail but the general pattern in the more complete statutes provides for a petition to a designated court; for notice to specified parties; for consent of natural parents or others; for investigations of the fitness of the child and of the proposed home; for report of investigation; for hearing and decrees, inter-

---

[1] *In re* Munch's Estate, 155 Misc. 836, 280 N. Y. Supp. 533 (Surr. Ct. 1935); Genz v. Riddle, 199 Wis. 545, 226 N. W. 957 (1929).

locutory in the event of a probation period, and final decree; and for appeal.

All the statutes specify who may adopt but in many jurisdictions the provisions are very indefinite, as "any proper person," "an inhabitant," "any resident," obviously leaving much to the discretion of the court. Variously expressed, twenty-four statutes require that the adopter be an adult, and sixteen specify that he must be "older" than the person adopted. Several statutes provide for adoption of or by nonresidents and a few states forbid adoption between the states, though exceptions are made in such states by persons who submit to the jurisdiction of the proper courts or who establish temporary residence. Four states have legislated against interracial adoption: Louisiana and Montana say that adopter and child must be of the same race; Nevada forbids Mongolian intermixture; and Texas prohibits Negro-white alliances. A number of states provide for the adoption of adults, but we are here interested only in the adoption of young children. Nor is it necessary to discuss the special provisions for adoption by or of relatives, step-parents or step-children, or by the father of his illegitimate child. In forty-four jurisdictions if the petitioner is married, husband or wife must join in the petition or consent to the adoption.

The first step in the court procedure is to file a petition in the proper court. Each statute specifies the court which has jurisdiction, usually probate, though sometimes the general court or a special court, as domestic relations or juvenile court. Its location depends upon residence in accordance with the general rule that domicile determines jurisdiction. At least half the statutes designate the county of the petitioner's residence, others specify the county of the child's residence or the county of the institution having guardianship or custody or where the child became a public charge. A number of statutes permit a choice between the counties of the petitioner's residence and the child's residence, and a very few designate the county of the natural parents' residence. Several states make special provision for court jurisdiction of adoption of or by nonresidents, as Maine, Massachusetts, New York, and Vermont, where petition is regularly made in the county of the petitioner's residence but if he is not a resident he may petition in the county of the child's residence; whereas in Missouri petition is usually made in the county of the child's residence but if he is not a resident it may be made in the petitioner's county. Whatever provision may be made for out-of-state adoptions, the difficulties and perhaps the dangers generally outweigh the advantages.

The form of the petition varies from no statutory requirements to a detailed list of specifications, such as names and addresses of the petitioners, and sometimes their ages or a statement of their ability to care for a child or their reasons for wishing to adopt; name, age, sex, and sometimes a statement about the property of the child, if he has any, and perhaps the new name by which they wish him to be known; names, ages, and occasionally consents of the natural parents, or an allegation that they are unknown or that the child is a ward of the state. The petition may contain any special terms, conditions, or benefits desired. So far as the validity of the adoption is concerned the actual form of the document is less important than the contents or the fact that there is or has been such a paper. Sample forms for petitions, decrees, and other documents will be found in the next chapter.

In practically all the states consent of the natural parents is required, or of the mother if the child is illegitimate. Some statutes make further provision for consent by other relatives; guardian; "next friend"; child welfare officer; or other designated person in the event of the parents' death, mental or moral unfitness, forfeiture of civil rights, or abandonment of the child. In several states consent of the divorced parent having custody is sufficient; in others a parent divorced for cruelty, adultery, desertion, or other specified cause is not required to give consent. Several states provide that parental consent is unnecessary after parents have relinquished their rights in favor of an institution, or have placed their child in an institution for adoption. The statutes are not always clear as to consent, or when parental consent is not required, particularly for a child placed in an institution, as is indicated by the relatively large number of court cases in which the validity of the adoption hinged upon consent, this being illustrated in at least fifty-three decisions in twenty-nine states over a twelve-year period. In a score or more of cases consent was deemed unnecessary for such reasons as abandonment, unknown residence, best interests of child.[2] In at least twenty-eight cases consent was required or the adoption was found not valid for lack of proper consent.[3] In some of these cases consent had been withheld by a parent or an institution because of some objection to the adoption. In others, problems arose over the form of consent or who should give it, or insufficient effort had been made to find the proper persons to give consent. In a few cases the validity of the adoption appeared to depend upon the form of consent. The statutes variously designate the form of consent as a part of the petition; in writing or in person, sometimes by separate examination at the hearing; in writing verified by oath, affidavit, or witnesses; and special arrangements for nonresidents. Many statutes require the consent of the child to his own adoption if he has reached a specified age, ranging from ten to seventeen years, the most common age being fourteen. Others leave the child's consent to the discretion of the court or of the investigating agency.

[2] McKenzie v. State Board of Control, 197 Minn. 234, 266 N. W. 746 (1936); *in re* Connolly, 154 Misc. 672, 278 N. Y. Supp. 32, (Surr. Ct. 1935).

[3] Rochford v. Bailey, 322 Mo. 1155, 17 S. W. (2d) 941 (1929); State v. District Court, 92 Mont. 411, 15 Pac. (2d) 238 (1932).

About one third of the statutes provide for notice to the
natural parents, by service or publication, if they have not
consented. Notice by publication ordinarily fulfills legal
requirements for such parents as fail to answer. A glance
at court cases for the last dozen years shows at least twenty-
seven decisions in sixteen states that appear to depend upon
notice to parents. Taken together with the previously mentioned cases hinging upon consent there were eighty decisions in thirty-one different states in which consent or notice
were deciding factors.

Often the court has sought to give the statutes a liberal
interpretation in order to protect the interests of the child
even though the letter of the law has not been followed.
There is evident a growing conviction, as voiced by the
courts, that adoption is desirable and should be encouraged,
not by making it easier but by safeguarding it so as to make
it satisfying and permanent. There is need for rethinking
and restatement of the provisions bearing upon consent,
which in a sense forms the basis for adoption and is essential
to its validity. Attention is called to the tables in Chapter
XI for further particulars, though they are incomplete due
to lack of space and sometimes to rather uncertain meaning
of the statutes.

The next legal step after the filing of the petition is the
action of the court upon it. In about half the jurisdictions
the statutes require a hearing before the granting of a decree.
In the others that formality is apparently not necessary
provided the proper consents have been secured and any
other requisites met. An unfortunate provision in a few
states—forcing adopters and natural parents to meet—is the
requirement that all the parties shall be present at the
hearing. Many statutes indicate that the court shall exercise
its discretion in allowing an adoption, in some such words as
that the court must be satisfied that the adoption is for the
best interests of the child or is "fit and proper," even in

states that do not require an investigation by a social agency or a court officer. Studies of court records indicate that many decrees are granted on the day the petition is made, which indicates a very superficial exercise of discretion as well as a need for more legislation for investigation and for trial residence.

As with the petition, the form and content of the decree vary considerably and are less important than the fact that the decree was granted. Many statutes omit all description of the decree, others designate a standard form or list the contents. A common statement regarding it is substantially this: "If the court is satisfied that the proposed adoption is for the best interests of the child, an order is made declaring such child to be from that date child and heir of said petitioner." Some of the states requiring a trial period of residence make an interlocutory decree awarding the care and custody of the child to the petitioners. This order, as compared with the final decree, is easily revocable by the petitioners, the natural parents, the court, the child welfare department, or other interested persons if the new relationship does not work out satisfactorily. Such an order does not constitute an adoption unless the final decree is made, except where the statute specifies that the temporary order becomes permanent after the trial period unless set aside. The final decree usually "sets forth the facts" of the adoption, including the change of name of the child, except in a few states where without formality he takes the name of the adopter. More often the new name forms a part of the petition and of the decree. In at least ten states the decree amounts to confirmation of the agreement which the petitioner must make or which the petitioners and consenters execute together. Some states issue a certified copy of the decree to be used as evidence. Whatever the details, the proceedings must be carried forward until the final decree is obtained, to which all previous steps are but preliminaries.

In the eyes of the law there is no adoption until the decree is entered.

As many as eighteen states make provision for annulment if the adoption does not prove satisfactory. The most used formula is: "within five years, if the child shows evidence of feeblemindedness, insanity, epilepsy, or venereal disease from causes existing at the time of the adoption and not then known to the adopting parent." Adequate investiga-tion and trial period would practically rule out such possibilities. The other main reasons for revocation are misrepresentation or fraud and the failure of the adopter in his duty to the child. One state permits annulment "for grave cause" but the statute adds that adoption is intended to be a permanent relation. There is substantial opinion that adoption should be final, for better or for worse, and revocation allowed only in extreme cases.[4] The adopter has recourse to the same aids as the natural parent if the child is unruly, mentally retarded, or ill, and there seems to be little reason why the adopter should not bear the full responsibility of a step voluntarily and deliberately taken. More thorough investigation and an enforced period of trial residence is wiser strategy than easy annulment.

Adoption is social birth. Once the decree has been made, the parents' obligation is in every sense as binding as if it grew out of blood lineage. If the adopters, acting in haste perhaps by side-stepping protective law and placement practice, find later that they do not want the child, their release from responsibility (annulment) is no more justified than it would be for an undesired own child.

Only about one third of the states provide for safeguarding the records of adoption from public inspection, and nearly one third make no mention of keeping the records at all. Again, we note that practice in some courts and social

[4] *In re* Zartman's Adoption, 334 Mo. 237, 65 S. W. (2d) 951 (1933); *in re* Anonymous, 157 Misc. 951, 285 N. Y. Supp. 827 (Surr. Ct. 1936).

agencies is better than the lagging laws require. However, in a matter so vital to the adoptive family there should be careful provision on every statute for keeping adoption records separate from other court business, and for guarding social records, such as reports of investigation and court testimony, from public inspection. To forestall any question of legality of the adoption, it is important that the legal records should be readily available, and not buried in unindexed matter. Added protection is given in the states which send a copy of the decree and court records to the state welfare department. A few states provide for a public record of the decree but keep reports of the case and of the investigation from public inspection or copy. This confidential treatment of the reports affords greater protection than certain other statutes which allow the judge in his discretion to impound the records or which exclude from the public records foundlings, illegitimate, or abandoned children. If only an occasional case is kept secret it may at least be inferred that there is something about it which needs to be hidden.

A number of statutes provide for the notification of the bureau of vital statistics of every adoption. The child's birth registration is then altered or rewritten, the original record filed and often sealed, and a copy of the new certificate, in the changed name of the child, is issued upon request of the adopters or of the child when he reaches his majority. Several states require that the new birth certificate shall not indicate that the child is adopted or whether or not he was legitimate.

We come now to what many statutes refer to as the effect of adoption, and what others call rights or status of the child, the adopters, and the natural parents. There is practically complete agreement, though variously expressed, that with the exception of inheritance, adopters and child shall have all rights, privileges, and obligations, and that all such ties shall be terminated between the child and his natural parents. In some states when this last point has arisen the courts have upheld the view that after a child is adopted he and his natural parents shall be strangers and that their relinquishment or consent to the adoption has taken away all their rights, even to see him.[5] A few states delineate certain rights of adopter and child, such as that the adopter has claim on the services, wages, control, and custody or company of the child; the child, to support and education. Most statutes leave to custom the definition of such parental-filial benefits.

As to inheritance of property, statutory provisions range from a simple statement that the child is heir or "legal child" of the adopters to complex limitations, allowances, and exceptions. Even where the wording of the law seems clear and unequivocal the court interpretations may vary from state to state, or even in different courts of the same state. In the face of such wide divergence of laws and of court decisions every adopter does well to safeguard his adopted child's inheritance by a specifically worded will or trust fund, not relying on such ambiguities as "child" or "issue" especially if any part of his property consists of land or may descend *through* the adoptive parent. It is helpful, in trying to understand the inheritance rights of adoptive families, to remember that the adoption statutes must be seen against the background of the much older laws of descent and distribution which may still operate if the adoption provisions are not clearly defined.

In eight jurisdictions the statutes do not mention inheritance, though in some states it may be inferred from such phrasing as that adopter and child "sustain toward each other the legal relation of parent and child" or that the

---

[5] People *ex rel.* Swasing v. Rebecca Talbot Perkins Adoption Society, Inc., 163 Misc. 719, 296 N. Y. Supp. 779, (Sup. Ct. 1937); Stickles v. Reichardt, 203 Wis. 579, 234 N. W. 728 (1931).

adopted child shall be "to all legal intents and purposes the child of the petitioner." The majority of the statutes expressly mention that the adopted child may inherit from his adoptive parents though a few say that such right may be limited by the decree or by the terms of consent, and over one fourth impose restrictions as to heirs of the body, forced heirs, or property from lineal or collateral adoptive relatives. If the property in question consists of real estate the adopted child cannot be certain of inheriting it, unless specified by will, even from his adoptive parents, particularly if the land is in some state other than that where the adoption took place.[6]

In at least twelve jurisdictions reciprocal inheritance is specified for adopter and child and in five others the adopter inherits from the child, with some restrictions in two states. Two more states forbid inheritance from the child by his adoptive parents, one if the child dies under age, and one prohibits inheritance by the adoptive father.

Most of the statutes are silent on questions of inheritance from adoptive relatives and in the absence of express provision the courts have tended to deny such rights to the adopted child, though in recent years a number of decisions have given him rights *through* as well as *from* his adoptive parents.[7] In five states the statutes provide that the adopted child may inherit from collateral adoptive relatives by representation and in six others that he may inherit from the legal descendants of his adoptive parents. In eight jurisdictions the child is denied the right to inherit from his lineal or collateral adoptive relatives, and in one more, from collateral adoptive relatives alone.

---

[6] Shaver v. Nash, 181 Ark. 1112, 29 S. W. (2d) 298 (1930); Frey v. Nielson, 99 N. J. Eq. 135, 132 Atl. 765 (1926).

[7] McCune v. Oldham, 213 Iowa 1221, 240 N. W. 678 (1932); Riemann v. Riemann, 124 Kan. 539, 262 Pac. 16 (1927); compare *in re* Cave's Estate, 326 Pa. 258, 192 Atl. 460 (1937) with *in re* Reamer's Estate, 315 Pa. 148, 172 Atl. 655 (1934).

Statutes in about a dozen jurisdictions give the adopted child the right to inherit from his natural parents, and in a few states, from other natural relatives, while in half that number he is denied such right. Some statutes give and others deny inheritance to natural parents. Most statutes have no provisions for inheritance by or from natural parents and many states have not decided the matter in the courts. The tendency seems to be for judicial decision to give inheritance both to and from natural parents in the absence of specific statutory provision in accord with the "call of the blood" in the old laws of succession.

It can be seen from this brief discussion and from a glance at the tables in the next chapter that the laws of inheritance for the adoptive family are chaotic and incomplete. In a few states, notably Pennsylvania, there is discernible an effort to make a complete substitution of inheritance rights from the natural to the adoptive family. This is in line with the accepted social theory of adoption as complete substitution for the natural family in every respect except the biological. The social scientist affirms that the essence of parenthood is sociological rather than merely physiological. Perhaps the full realization of this is too much to expect of legislators devoted to the land-lineage and blood-lineage traditions in the more conservative parts of the country. Certainly the adoption statutes touching inheritance need redrafting in almost every state. At present the courts are left to flounder in a nearly uncharted sea. In the period 1926–1937 there were eighty-seven court decisions in thirty-two states involving inheritance in adoptive families. All of the leading cases for that period concerning adoption had to do with consent or inheritance or both.

Confusing as are the statutory differences of the several states to an increasingly mobile population, yet even more involved becomes the adoption in which the laws of a foreign country or international law are implicated. Nationality is no longer the simple concept of birth into a tribe and subsequent allegiance to it. Under the development of nationalism it has come to be based on the claims of nations, enforced by international law. In general the adopted child assumes the nationality of his adoptive parents but if he was born in a foreign country or if his parents were foreign-born he may have a dual nationality. Our laws regarding the nationality of children are now under scrutiny and bills clarifying the citizenship status of adopted as well as illegitimate children and foundlings have been proposed.

There is a growing interest in adoption today. Adoption laws are being strengthened with a recognition of social qualities and values. Every person intelligently interested in this field helps to shape public opinion toward a demand for and an acceptance of improved methods.

Strict compliance with the statutes is indispensable because legally adoption is an artificial process whose only foundation is statutory. To neglect, postpone, or overconfidently dismiss any step in that process is to endanger the validity of the adoptive relationship. Efforts of sociologists, social workers, physicians, psychologists, and other assisting specialists are valuable and desirable but compliance with law is fundamental; nevertheless, all these must work together to lift the law to a higher social level.

II

Adoption Statutes

This chapter shows at a glance in condensed form the adoption statutes for all jurisdictions of the United States as they stood at the end of 1938. From a social viewpoint, the tabulation classifies the statutes which should be of primary interest to the adopter or the child welfare worker. Such a state by state comparison may also be useful to students, legislators, and others. In this simplified map of adoption for the nation and its possessions, we have traced only the main highways. At times we have reduced the wording of the law to simple terms for purposes of general introductory guidance.

The more technical legal points, such as must be complied with to make the adoption valid, revolve about who may make the petition and where it must be presented; who must consent to the adoption and in what manner; and the hearing and decree. Those social aspects which do not affect the validity of the adoption but which do safeguard it as a permanent and satisfactory type of family life are as follows: the investigation, of whom and by what means; the trial period; the records, what they contain and how they are kept; and the status or effect of the adoption, that is, the legal relationship between adopter and child, including inheritance of property.

These are by no means all the questions that arise nor is there any attempt here to include all the details as they appear in the laws. No tabular mention has been made of such matters as the following: the adoption of adults, adoption by a step-parent, unusual exceptions and provisions for consent, and certain points related to nonresident adoption. Because of lack of space we have concentrated upon those things that seem to be of most value for the adoptive family. Rather than limit the citations of codes and laws to the precise adoption statutes, we have included a few provisions sometimes found under other headings yet pertinent to adoption, such as mention of altered birth certificates and certain rights of inheritance.

The laws in connection with child welfare generally, and particularly those having to do with adoption, are changing fairly rapidly. The table will invite alterations as the laws are amended. Some of these changes in the years ahead will be of minor importance; others will be socially significant. Progressive states, whose social welfare practice is to give more protection for children and parents than the law requires, are increasingly emphasizing more thorough investigation of home and child with a view to selective placement, more mental examinations, and longer trial periods. It is likely, in view of the trend, that within the next decade constructive legislation will be accelerated in states now lagging.

A glance across the tabular pages may reveal all the columns with impressive-looking content or it may show up a number of blank spaces. It should be kept in mind that laws on books do not necessarily mean their wise application. For example, investigation, so very important, may be quite inadequate despite legal provision. On the other hand, a state with a few simple, yet flexible laws with liberal interpretations—like the family with few rules but with much co-operative *esprit de corps*—may have excellence in adoption practices. Nevertheless, it must be said that the aggregate of blank spaces on the social side, especially under

NOTE: *The legal and social steps by which the petitioner advisedly proceeds toward the adoption of a child are suggested by the numbers heading each column*

| STATE | 1. PETITION PRESENTED | | 4. MUST HAVE CONSENT OF | 6. DECREE |
	BY WHOM?	WHERE?		
ALABAMA Ala. Code Ann. (*Michie*, *Supp. 1936*) § 9302.	Any proper adult person, or husband-wife jointly	Probate court in county of residence of child, or petitioner	Parents; mother if child illegitimate; guardian; State Child Welfare Dept. Child if over 14	Interlocutory, revocable, for custody, name. Final after one year residence
ALASKA Alaska Comp. Laws (*1933*) §§ 1141–1151.	Any inhabitant of the territory	To commissioner in precinct of child's residence	Parents; guardian; next of kin; application to court if a parent insane or imprisoned	
ARIZONA Ariz. Rev. Code Ann. (*Struckmeyer*, *1928*) §§ 117–120, 125–6; (*Courtright*, *Supp. 1936*) §§ 121–124.	Person at least ten years older than child; husband-wife jointly	Superior court in county of child's residence	Parents; guardian; next of kin; next friend. If they do not consent, notice published 3 weeks in county paper	Interlocutory, revocable. Final order entered on interlocutory decree after one year's residence. Name changed
ARKANSAS Ark. Dig. Stat. (*Pope*, *1937*) §§ 254–271. Ark. Sess. Laws 1937, act 41, § 7(2).	Any person; husband-wife jointly	Probate court in county of residence of child, or of petitioner	Parents; mother if child illegitimate; guardian; child if over 14. Must appear in court, file written consents, verified, or affidavit	Sets forth facts, name changed. Final after two years if parent-child relation continues
CALIFORNIA Cal. Civ. Code (*Deering*, *1937*) §§ 221–230; Cal. Prob. Code (*Deering*, *1937*) § 257.	Adult resident at least ten years older than child; husband or wife must consent	Superior court in county of petitioner's residence	Parents (mother if child illegitimate) with exceptions, unless relinquished to placing agency. Child if over 12	Order after written agreement

SOCIAL ASPECTS
(to 1938)

NOTE: *The provisions here are no less statutory than those on the opposite page but they are essentially social in their meaning. The italics in Column 3 indicate investigation initiated by courts that may or may not have full social welfare emphasis*

3. SOCIAL INVESTIGATION	5. TRIAL PERIOD	7. RECORDS	8. STATUS AND INHERITANCE RIGHTS
By State Child Welfare Dept. covering such matters as to why child is available, as to petitioner's moral and financial fitness, as to physical and mental fitness of the child	One year	Of petition, decree, in special indexed book. Records open to inspection or copy only to parties in interest or State Child Welfare Dept. except on court order. New birth certificate. Decree and original birth certificate sealed by Bureau Vital Statistics	Adopter and child have all parent-child rights and obligations, including inheritance. Child adopted elsewhere may inherit in Alabama. Natural parents and child have no rights or obligations. Child may inherit from them
			Child has rights of a natural child except cannot inherit by representation of adopter or property limited to heirs of the body
By an officer of the court or by public welfare agent (otherwise similar to Alabama)	One year	Files, records open only to parties in interest or a public welfare official except on court order	Child is heir at law of the adopters, entitled to all rights, privileges; subject to all obligations of an own child. Natural parents are divested of all rights
By State Dept. Public Welfare covering such matters as to why child is available, petitioner's financial fitness, mental and physical fitness of child, etc.	Six months	Report to State Dept. Public Welfare. Records open to inspection or copy only on court order except to parties in interest or to State Dept. Pub. Welfare. Report to registrar vital statistics; copy of record of adoption on request	Adopter-adoptee have all parent-child rights. Child may inherit real or personal property from adopter. Inherits from natural parent. Natural parents, no rights
By State Dept. of Social Welfare of petitioner and child if not placed by an authorized agency		All papers filed in county clerk's office; seen only on court order except to parties in interest. Decree filed with old birth certificate in Bureau Vital Statistics. New birth certificate does not mention adoption	Legal parent-child relation. Reciprocal inheritance. Child may take adopter's surname. Rights of natural parents terminated. No inheritance by or from natural parents

NOTE: *The legal and social steps by which the petitioner advisedly proceeds toward the adoption of a child are suggested by the numbers heading each column.*

| STATE | 1. PETITION PRESENTED | | 4. MUST HAVE CONSENT OF | 6. DECREE |
	BY WHOM?	WHERE?		
CANAL ZONE CANAL ZONE CODE (1934) tit. 3, §§ 191–196.	Any adult resident; husband-wife jointly. Guardian may not adopt until court terminates guardianship	District court	Parents, guardian, person appointed by court, or head of agency where child is. Child if over 14	"When Court is satisfied." Sets forth facts. Name changed
COLORADO COLO. STAT. ANN. (Michie, 1935)c. 4, §§ 1–5, c. 9, § 31, c. 78, §§ 118–119, 146.	Any inhabitant of state; husband-wife jointly. Wife must consent	Juvenile or district or county court in county of residence of petitioner or child	Parents, guardian, next friend, conservator. Head of institution where child is or board of control. Child if over 14	"If Court is satisfied." Sets forth facts. New name of child
CONNECTICUT CONN. GEN. STAT. (Supp. 1935) §§1580c–1581c; (Supp. 1937) § 104d.	Any person of full age; husband-wife jointly	Probate court in district of guardian's or petitioner's residence	Parents, guardian, selectmen, board of managers of orphan's home. Child if over 14	"If Court finds it for welfare of child and for public interest"
DELAWARE DEL. REV. CODE (1935) §§ 3550–3552; Del. Sess. Laws 1937, c. 187.	Any resident over 21; husband-wife jointly	Orphan's court in county of petitioner's residence	Parents, guardian, next friend. Child if over 14	Interlocutory, revocable. Final after one year, must be entered
DISTRICT OF COLUMBIA D.C. CODE (Supp. 1937) tit. 18, § 61.	Adult resident for one year; husband-wife jointly or consent	District court	Parents, mother if child illegitimate. Child if over 14	Interlocutory becomes final in six months unless set aside. Name changed when decree is entered; adoptee takes name of adopter unless decree provides otherwise
FLORIDA FLA. COMP. GEN. LAWS ANN. (Skillman, 1927) §§ 5076–5081, 5488, (Supp. 1936) § 5480 (8).	Any person	Circuit court in circuit of petitioner's residence		By judge "in his discretion"

142

SOCIAL ASPECTS
(to 1938)

NOTE: *The provisions here are no less statutory than those on the opposite page but they are essentially social in their meaning. The italics in Column 3 indicate investigation initiated by courts that may or may not have full social welfare emphasis*

3. SOCIAL INVESTIGATION	5. TRIAL PERIOD	7. RECORDS	8. STATUS AND INHERITANCE RIGHTS
			Child has all rights including inheritance. Rights of natural parents terminated
		Adopter may have a certificate of identification in lieu of a birth certificate for the child	Child is legal heir of adopters. Adoptive family inherits from child. Natural parents divested of all rights
		Order recorded and indexed under names of petitioner and child. Birth certificate altered to show date of adoption; copies only to petitioner or child when of age	"Legal child," inherits from adopters, not from parents. Adopters inherit from child
By State Board of Charities covering mutual suitability of child and parents; written report within 60 days, and other points similar to Alabama	One year	Copy of certificate of adoption sent to State Board Charities. Change of child's name reported to registrar of vital statistics	Child's name changed from the entry of interlocutory order. Inheritance from adopters. Natural parents divested of rights
By Board of Public Welfare or report accepted from social, charitable, or religious agency	Six months	Papers, records, docket sealed. Opened only by court order for extraordinary cause. Court may permit parties in interest or Board of Public Welfare to inspect while proceedings are pending	Child is heir of adopter. Inherits from but not through. Adopters and their collaterals inherit from child. Natural parents, no rights
		Order recorded in circuit court	Child is heir of adopter, also inherits from natural kin but they not from him. Adopter inherits from child. Child adopted in another state may inherit in Florida

STATUTORY ASPECTS
(to 1938)

NOTE: *The legal and social steps by which the petitioner advisedly proceeds toward the adoption of a child are suggested by the numbers heading each column*

STATE	1. PETITION PRESENTED		4. MUST HAVE CONSENT OF	6. DECREE
	BY WHOM?	WHERE?		
GEORGIA GA. CODE (1933) §§ 74-401—74-406.	Resident of state 25 years old or married; ten years older than child. Husband-wife jointly	Superior court of county where child is domiciled	Parents. Next of kin must be summoned and may object, but need not consent. Child if over 14	Granted on second hearing after six months trial. Changes name of child
HAWAII HAWAII REV. LAWS (1935) §§ 4520–4527.	Any proper person. Husband-wife jointly	Circuit court in circuit of residence of petitioner or child	Parents, guardian, next friend. Child if over 16. Summons, publication for 4 weeks if parents not found	"If judge satisfied." Order states facts, changes name of child
IDAHO IDAHO CODE ANN. (1932) §§ 31-1101—31-1109.	Any adult at least 15 years older than child. Husband-wife jointly	Probate court in county of petitioner's residence	Parents, guardian, relative. Child if over 12	"If court satisfied." Petitioner makes agreement. Name changed
ILLINOIS ILL. REV. STAT. (Smith-Hurd, 1937) c. 4, §§ 1-12.	Any respectable person. Husband-wife jointly	Circuit court or county court in county of petitioner's residence or where child is found	Parents, guardian, custodian, near relative. Notice published if residence unknown. Child if over 14	Sets forth facts, change of name
INDIANA IND. STAT. ANN. (Burns, 1933) §§ 3-101—3-114.	Any person	Circuit court of county where child resides	Parents in court or consent verified; board of managers of institution where child is committed, or board of control	"When court satisfied." Name changed

144

SOCIAL ASPECTS
(to 1938)

NOTE: *The provisions here are no less statutory than those on the opposite page but they are essentially social in their meaning. The italics in Column 3 indicate investigation initiated by courts that may or may not have full social welfare emphasis*

3. SOCIAL INVESTIGATION	5. TRIAL PERIOD	7. RECORDS	8. STATUS AND INHERITANCE RIGHTS
	Six months	Decree filed with registrar of vital statistics	Adopter-adoptee relationship as of parent and child except that the adoptive father cannot inherit from the child
			Adopter-adoptee have legal parent-child relationship; child inherits from adopters, not from natural parents; adopter inherits from child, natural parents do not inherit
			Adopter-adoptee have all parent-child rights and duties. Natural parents, no rights
		Certified record filed with clerk of court. Birth certificate changed, one copy to State Dept. Health, one to local registrar, one to county clerk. Each shall make permanent record and issue copy of certificate on request. All certificates shall be uniform in size, color, ink; not to state that child is adopted, legitimate, or illegitimate	Adoptee has rights of natural child of adopters including inheritance, with some exceptions. Adoptive family inherits from child only such property as came from adoptive family. Natural parents, no rights
			Child has rights of natural child including inheritance and if he leaves no heirs his property goes to his adoptive kin. Child adopted in another state has all rights if adoption records filed in a circuit court of Indiana

NOTE: *The legal and social steps by which the petitioner advisedly proceeds toward the adoption of a child are suggested by the numbers heading each column*

| STATE | 1. PETITION PRESENTED | | 4. MUST HAVE CONSENT OF | 6. DECREE |
	BY WHOM?	WHERE?		
IOWA Iowa Code (1935 §§ 10501–b1—10501–b8, 12017, 12027–12028. Iowa Sess. Laws 1937, c. 118, § 11.	Any person of lawful age. Husband-wife jointly	Any court of record in county where child or petitioner resides	Parents, guardian, with exceptions; subdivision of Child Welfare of the State Board of Social Welfare. Child if over 14	"If court satisfied." Sets forth facts, changes child's name, if desired. Certified copy given to adopters
KANSAS Kan. Gen. Stat. Ann. (Corrick, 1935) §§ 38–105—38–107, 38–114, 38–117, 38–118.	Any person or persons	Probate court in county of petitioner's residence	Parents, mother if child is illegitimate, parent having custody if they are divorced; guardian, must appear in court or send affidavits if nonresident. Children's home that has custody of child	Court has authority "to make an order declaring" adoptee heir at law of petitioner
KENTUCKY Ky. Stat. Ann. (Carroll, 1936) §§ 2071–2072b.	Anyone 21 years of age; husband-wife jointly	Circuit court in county of petitioner's residence	Parents, mother if child is illegitimate, an institution to which the child has been committed for a year or more	Shows name, age, birthplace, new name of child, names of parents and adopters. Court may allow or establish terms of contract.
LOUISIANA La. Laws 1938, act 428.	Any person over age 21 may adopt a child under age 17 of same race; husband-wife jointly	Juvenile or district court in parish of residence of petitioner or child	Parents; custodian, with exceptions	Interlocutory for six months; final only after child has lived with petitioner for one year, if court satisfied. Name changed
MAINE Me. Rev. Stat. (1930) c. 80, §§ 35–41; Me. Pub. Laws 1935, c. 48, 49.	Any unmarried person or husband-wife jointly	Probate court in county of petitioner's residence. If a nonresident, in county where child lives	Parents or the one having custody, if divorced; guardian, next of kin in the state; next friend. Child if over 14	Sets forth facts, name changed with no public notice

SOCIAL ASPECTS
(to 1938)

NOTE: *The provisions here are no less statutory than those on the opposite page but they are essentially social in their meaning. The italics in Column 3 indicate investigation initiated by courts that may or may not have full social welfare emphasis*

3. SOCIAL INVESTIGATION	5. TRIAL PERIOD	7. RECORDS	8. STATUS AND INHERITANCE RIGHTS
Court investigates child's antecedents, petitioner's home, etc.	Six months	Findings of court filed in complete record and a duplicate copy sent to subdivision of child welfare for their files	As between parents and children in lawful wedlock, including inheritance. Adoptive parents and kin take from the child but if there are no adoptive heirs property goes to natural heirs
By court which may refuse petition		Consent to be recorded in the journal	Child has same rights of person and property as an own child
			Decree gives "parental control." Surname may be changed by special petition. Adopters inherit from child except such property as came from his blood kin
By State Board of Public Welfare through the Bureau of Child Welfare. Inquiry covers moral and financial fitness of adopters, health conditions of home, adjustment of child and suitability of child for the home. Petitioner certified by State Dept. Public Welfare	One year	Records filed separately with special indexes opened only on court order except to parties in interest. Certified copy to Bureau of Vital Statistics; new birth certificate; old birth certificate sealed and filed, open only to parties in interest, State Dept. Public Welfare, or on court order	"Upon entry of final order of adoption, the said child shall cease to be heir of its parents . . . and shall at the same time become an heir of its adoptive parents to the extent provided by existing law"
At request of court by bureau of public welfare	Court may require one year	Attested copy filed with State Bureau of Vital Statistics	Child inherits from adopters unless otherwise provided in the decree with some exceptions. Property from adopters goes to adoptive kin; that from natural parents to natural kin

NOTE: *The legal and social steps by which the petitioner advisedly proceeds toward the adoption of a child are suggested by the numbers heading each column*

STATE	1. PETITION PRESENTED		4. MUST HAVE CONSENT OF	6. DECREE
	BY WHOM?	WHERE?		
MARYLAND M D. C O D E ANN. (*Bagby, 1924*) art. 16, §§ 74–79; Md. Sess. Laws 1935, c. 63.	Resident of county or city. Husband or wife must consent	Equity court in county or city of residence of petitioner or child	(Notice to parents or guardian by summons or publication)	Name changed if petitioned for
MASSACHU– SETTS MASS. ANN. LAWS (*1933*) c. 210, §§ 1–11A, c. 119. §§ 14, 16, 30A.	Person of full age; husband-wife jointly	Probate court in county where petitioner lives or if nonresident, where child resides	Parents, mother of illegitimate child, board public welfare if child is public charge, guardian *ad litem.* Child if over 14	"If Court satisfied." Name changed if petitioned for
MICHIGAN MICH. STAT. ANN. (*1938*) §§ 27–3150 to 27–3155.	Any person or persons	Judge of probate court in county of petitioner's residence	Parents, mother if child is illegitimate, guardian, supt. or county agent of public welfare if child is inmate of the State School	Order authorizes petition
MINNESOTA MINN. STAT. (*Mason, 1927*) §§ 8624–8632.	Any resident; husband-wife jointly	District court in county where petitioner resides	Parents, mother if child is illegitimate, guardian, State Dept. Public Welfare, supt. of State School if child is ward. Child if over 14	"If Court satisfied." Name changed
MISSISSIPPI MISS. CODE ANN. (*1930*) § 358; Miss. Gen. Laws 1938, c. 268, 269.	Any person	Chancery court in county of petitioner's residence, or in which person to be adopted resides	Parents, guardian join in petition or are summoned. Child if over 14	"If Court satisfied." Name changed if prayed for in the petition

SOCIAL ASPECTS
(to 1938)

NOTE: *The provisions here are no less statutory than those on the opposite page but they are essentially social in their meaning. The italics in Column 3 indicate investigation initiated by courts that may or may not have full social welfare emphasis*

3. SOCIAL INVESTIGATION	5. TRIAL PERIOD	7. RECORDS	8. STATUS AND INHERITANCE RIGHTS
To satisfy court			Child has same rights of care and inheritance as if born to adopters. His property is distributed as the lawful child of the adopters except as he wills it. A person adopted in another state has Maryland rights upon proof of adoption
By dept. of public welfare; investigates child's antecedents, petitioner's home, with due regard to race and religion, etc.	Six months unless waived by the court	Report of investigation filed apart from other papers in case, subject to inspection only on court order. Illegitimacy not averred upon the record	Child inherits from adopters but from no other adoptive kin; may inherit from natural kin. Name changed. Child is "as if natural child" except for rights of succession
By county agent or probation officer in writing as to consents, character, ability, etc.		Instrument filed in probate court, order of adoption entered on journal	Adopters stand in place of parents to child who shall be their heir at law. Adopters inherit from child
By State Board of Control to determine fitness of child and suitability of foster home, similar to Alabama	Six months	Copy of decree mailed to State Board of Control in twenty days. Records open to inspection or copy only to parties in interest	Adoptee becomes "legal child" of the adopter with all rights and duties. His estate goes to his adoptive family
		Bureau of Vital Statistics shall change birth certificate of child to "show names of adoptive parents in lieu of names of natural parents." New name of child displaces prior name	Child is entitled to all benefits proposed by the adopter, who has "all such power and control as parents have over their own children"

STATUTORY ASPECTS
(to 1938)

NOTE: *The legal and social steps by which the petitioner advisedly proceeds toward the adoption of a child are suggested by the numbers heading each column*

STATE	1. PETITION PRESENTED BY WHOM?	2. PETITION PRESENTED WHERE?	4. MUST HAVE CONSENT OF	6. DECREE
MISSOURI Mo. Stat. Ann. (*Supp. 1935*) §§ 14073–14080.	Any respectable person; husband-wife jointly	Juvenile division of circuit court in county where child resides. If child is nonresident, in county of petitioner's residence	Parents, guardian, institution having custody of child. Child if over 14	"If Court satisfied." Name changed
MONTANA Mont. Rev. Codes Ann. (*Anderson & McFarland, 1935*) §§ 5856–5867.	Any U. S. citizen at least 10 years older than child; of same race as child. Husband or wife must consent	District court in county where petitioner resides	Parents, mother if child is illegitimate, trustees of orphan asylum. Child if over 12	Order authorizes the petitioner's agreement to treat child as his own
NEBRASKA Neb. Comp. Stat. (*1929*) §§ 43–101— 43–112, 71–2508, 71–2511, 71–2512; Neb. comp.stat. (*Supp. 1937*) §§ 83–504.	Any adult; husband or wife must consent	County court in county of petitioner's residence	Parents, mother if child is illegitimate; person or institution having custody for preceding 6 months; guardian. Child if over 14	In accordance with terms of consent
NEVADA Nev. Comp. Laws (*Hillyer, 1929*) §§ 9475– 9485; Nev. Stat. 1933, c. 16.	Any adult at least 10 years older than child. Husband-wife jointly or consent. Mongolians may adopt only a Mongolian child	District court in county of petitioner's residence	Parents, mother if child is illegitimate. President of orphan asylum having custody of child	Order authorizing agreement of petitioner to treat child as his own "lawful child"
NEW HAMPSHIRE N. H. Pub. Laws (*1926*) c. 292, §§ 1–7; N. H. Pub. Laws 1937, c. 143, § 10.	Any inhabitant. Husband-wife jointly. Nonresident may adopt	Probate court in county of residence of petitioner or child	Parents, mother if child is illegitimate; next of kin in state; guardian, next friend. Child if over 14	Sets forth facts, changes name if in petition

SOCIAL ASPECTS
(to 1938)

NOTE: *The provisions here are no less statutory than those on the opposite page but they are essentially social in their meaning. The italics in Column 3 indicate investigation initiated by courts that may or may not have full social welfare emphasis*

3. SOCIAL INVESTIGATION	5. TRIAL PERIOD	7. RECORDS	8. STATUS AND INHERITANCE RIGHTS
			Adopter is "entitled to services, wages, control, custody and company of said child." Reciprocal inheritance except such as is limited to heirs of the body. Custody not transferable. Natural parents, no rights
			Adopter has all rights and duties. Child may take family name of adopter. Natural parents, no rights
		Records kept in book for the purpose, known as the Adoption Record. Decree entered	As a child born to the adopters unless terms are stated
		Order entered in minutes of the court. Papers filed. Certified copies filed, recorded in office of county recorder, "such records shall be notice to the world of such adoption"	Child takes family name of the adopter who has all rights and duties of a parent including support, protection and inheritance. Natural parents, have rights
Judge may cause investigation and report by probation officer			Child has same relation to adoptive parents and kin in respect to inheritance and all other incidents as if he were born to them, except for property limited to heirs of the body. Property from his natural family returns to it, not to the adoptive family. Adopter may not inherit from minor adopted child

STATUTORY ASPECTS
(to 1938)

NOTE: *The legal and social steps by which the petitioner advisedly proceeds toward the adoption of a child are suggested by the numbers heading each column*

STATE	1. PETITION PRESENTED — BY WHOM?	2. PETITION PRESENTED — WHERE?	4. MUST HAVE CONSENT OF	6. DECREE
NEW JERSEY N. J. Rev. Stat. (1937) §§ 9: 3–1; N. J. Rev. Stat. (Supp. 1938) §§ 9: 3–2—9: 3–11.	A citizen of United States at least 21 years old and 10 years older than child. Husband-wife jointly or consent	Orphan's court in county of residence of child or petitioner	Parents, guardian, next friend; institution having custody of child. Consent written and acknowledged like deeds of land. Child if over 14	If court satisfied; entry is evidence; name changed
NEW MEXICO N. M. Stat. Ann. (Courtright, 1929) §§ 2-101—2-116.	Any adult 10 years older than child. Husband-wife must consent. Charitable organization for care of orphans or other children in its care	District court in county of petitioner's residence	Parents, mother if child is illegitimate, parent having custody if they are separated. Consent waived if mother a prostitute or if child is abandoned. Child if over 12	Order authorizes agreement of petitioner to treat child with kindness and give him proper care and education
NEW YORK N. Y. Cons. Laws (Cahill, Supp. 1938) c. 14 §§ 109–113.	Adult; husband-wife jointly, must be adults	Children's court judge, county judge, or surrogate of county of residence of petitioner	Parents, mother if child is illegitimate, authorized custodian. Child if over 14	Name changed if no reasonable objection. Order confirming agreement and change of name
NORTH CAROLINA N. C. Code Ann. (Michie, 1935) §§ 191 (1)-191 (12), §§ 5067(i)-5067(p); N. C. Pub. Laws 1937, c. 422, § 1.	Any proper adult resident; husband-wife jointly	Superior court in county of residence of petitioner, or of child	Parent, guardian, custodian	Tentative approval gives care and custody. Final decree retroactive to date of application

SOCIAL ASPECTS
(to 1938)

3. SOCIAL INVESTIGATION	5. TRIAL PERIOD	7. RECORDS	8. STATUS AND INHERITANCE RIGHTS
By Dept. of Agencies, etc., except when child is under its custody; investigates child's antecedents, etc.	One year	Petition, decree, written testimony and proceedings recorded in indexed book kept for the purpose. Files open to inspection or copy only on court order	Child has every legal right including inheritance except property limited to heirs of the body or from collateral kin of the adopters. Inherits from natural kin. If adopters have other children, born and adopted inherit from and through each other
By State Board of Public Welfare within six months, report in writing for or against the adoption	Six months		Child takes family name of adopters and inherits from them. Natural parents lose all rights
Must be by authorized agency or by the court. Special protective measures if adoption not handled by authorized agency	Six months	Record and report *must* be sealed and opened only on court order and with notice to adoptive parents. Fact of illegitimacy not to appear on the record	Adopter-adoptee have all parent-child rights and duties including reciprocal inheritance with some exceptions. When more than one child is adopted they inherit as brothers and sisters. Child inherits from natural parents. Natural parents lose all rights
By county supt. of public welfare or representative of a placing agency. Written report sent directly to court; need not be disclosed	One year (within two years)	Petition filed in duplicate, one copy in court, one copy by State Board Charities and Public Welfare. Court reports to Bureau Vital Statistics which issues new birth certificate with no reference to adoption. Original birth registration a part of the record of the bureau. Order recorded in book for the purpose, copy to State Board Charities and Public Welfare	Adopter-adoptee have parent-child relationship for the minority of the child or for life, as petition states. If for life the child inherits as would an own child unless petition states otherwise. (If child has property, a bond is required of the adopters)

NOTE: *The legal and social steps by which the petitioner advisedly proceeds toward the adoption of a child are suggested by the numbers heading each column*

STATE	1. PETITION PRESENTED		4. MUST HAVE CONSENT OF	6. DECREE
	BY WHOM?	WHERE?		
NORTH DAKOTA N. D. Comp. Laws Ann. (Supp. 1925) §§ 4441–4450.	Any adult at least 10 years older than child, husband or wife must consent	District or county court in county of petitioner's residence	Parents, mother if child is illegitimate, guardian, Board of Administration. Child if over 10	"If court satisfied"
OHIO Ohio Gen. Code Ann. (Page, Supp. 1935)§§10512–9—10512–21; Ohio Gen. Code Ann. (Page, Supp. 1937) §§ 1352–12—1352–14.	Any proper person, husband-wife jointly (examined separately)	Probate court in county of petitioner's residence, or of child	Parents, mother if child is illegitimate, parent having custody if they are divorced, guardian, next friend, institution having custody. Child if over 13	"If court satisfied." Cites facts at length; name changed
OKLAHOMA Okla. Stat. Ann. (1936) tit. 10, §§ 41–56.	Any adult at least 10 years older than child. Husband-wife jointly or consent	County court in county of petitioner's residence	Parents, mother if child is illegitimate. Consent waived if no kin can be found to give it. Child if over 12.	"If court satisfied" after separate examination. Petitioner executes agreement
OREGON Ore. Code Ann. (1930) §§ 33–402—33–413; Ore. Code Ann. (Supp. 1935) §§ 33–401, 33–414—33–417.	Any person; husband-wife jointly	County court in county where petitioner resides or if nonresident, where parent or guardian of child resides	Parents, parent having custody if they are divorced; mother if child is illegitimate, guardian, next friend. Child if over 14	"If court is satisfied." Changes name, with other proceedings

SOCIAL ASPECTS
(to 1938)

NOTE: *The provisions here are no less statutory than those on the opposite page but they are essentially social in their meaning. The italics in Column 3 indicate investigation initiated by courts that may or may not have full social welfare emphasis*

3. SOCIAL INVESTIGATION	5. TRIAL PERIOD	7. RECORDS	8. STATUS AND INHERITANCE RIGHTS
By Board of Administration to inquire into conditions and antecedents, etc.	Six months	Records, files open to inspection or copy only on court order except to parties in interest	Child is "deemed as respects all legal consequences and incidents" the child of the adopter, including right to Workmen's Compensation. Natural parents, no rights
Court may authorize a representative of State Board of Charities to look into suitability of child and home	Six months	Petition, decree, proceedings in indexed book for the purpose, as a part of the court records. Reports filed	Child as if born to adopters, with some limitations of inheritance. Children by birth and adoption inherit from and through each other. Adoptee inherits from natural parent
			Child takes family name of adopter and is as if born to him except for property limited to heirs of the body or from lineal or collateral kin. Inheritance by the adoptive family from the child only such property as he has taken from or through them. Natural parents, nor rights
By State Child Welfare Commission within thirty days regarding status of child and suitability of the proposed home			Child inherits as if born to adopters except property limited to heirs of the body and from lineal or collateral kin

155

STATUTORY ASPECTS
(to 1938)

NOTE: *The legal and social steps by which the petitioner advisedly proceeds toward the adoption of a child are suggested by the numbers heading each column*

STATE	1. PETITION PRESENTED		4. MUST HAVE CONSENT OF	6. DECREE
	BY WHOM?	WHERE?		
PENNSYL- VANIA Pa. Stat. (*Purdon, 1936*) *tit. 1, §§ 1–5, tit. 20, §§ 101– 102, 211.*	Any adult citizen; hus- band or wife must consent	Orphan's court in county of res- idence of pe- titioner or of child	Parents, mother if child is illegitimate; guardian; custodian; previous adopters. Child if over 12	"If court is satis- fied." Name changed if desired
PHILIPPINE ISLANDS P. I. Code Civ. Proc. (*1901*) §§ *765–772; Phil- ippine Pub. Laws 1933, act 3977.*	Any inhabit- ant; hus- band-wife jointly	Court of First Instance	Parents, guardian. Child if over 14	"If court satisfied." Name changed
PUERTO RICO P. R. Civ. Code (*1930*) §§ *130–141.*	Person over 37 and 18 years older than child; with no le- gitimate chil- dren and not guardian of adoptee. Husband- wife jointly	District court	Parents, guardian, tutor. Male child if over 16, female over 14	Expresses condi- tions, changes name of child to that of adopter
RHODE ISLAND R. I. Gen. Laws (*1923*) c. *288, §§ 1– 10; R. I. Laws 1926, c. 852; R. I. Laws 1930, c. 1573.*	Any person older than child. Hus- band-wife jointly	Municipal court or pro- bate court of petitioner's town or of child's resi- dence	Parents, next kin, guardian, next friend. Child if over 14	"If court satisfied." Name changed if petitioned for, cer- tificate granted

SOCIAL ASPECTS
(to 1938)

NOTE: *The provisions here are no less statutory than those on the opposite page but they are essentially social in their meaning. The italics in Column 3 indicate investigation initiated by courts that may or may not have full social welfare emphasis*

3. SOCIAL INVESTIGATION	5. TRIAL PERIOD	7. RECORDS	8. STATUS AND INHERITANCE RIGHTS
Court may designate an investigator		Decree filed and recorded, open to public as evidence of the adoption. All other papers and records filed, may in discretion of judge be withheld from inspection	Child may take adopter's name if desired. Reciprocal inheritance as fully as if adoptee were lawful child. From and through. No inheritance from or by natural parents. Will of adopters revoked by subsequent adoption to allow child to inherit. Foreign adoptions valid
			Child takes name of adopter, inherits from them, also from natural parents. Property inherited from adopters returns to adoptive kin
		Decree is recorded in Civil Registry	Adoptee enjoys rights of legitimate child except that he cannot alter the rights of forced heirs. He retains rights from his natural family. Adopter and adoptee owe each other support
By Society for the Prevention of Cruelty to Children or State Public Welfare Commission	Six months		Adoptee inherits as natural child except property limited to heirs of the body or from lineal and collateral kin. Natural parents deprived of rights

STATUTORY ASPECTS
(to 1938)

NOTE: *The legal and social steps by which the petitioner advisedly proceeds toward the adoption of a child are suggested by the numbers heading each column*

STATE	1. PETITION PRESENTED		4. MUST HAVE CONSENT OF	6. DECREE
	BY WHOM?	WHERE?		
SOUTH CAROLINA S. C. CODE (1932) § 8679.	Any person (wife must consent if mother of the child. Involved restrictions on adoption of illegitimate child)	Court of common pleas in county where petitioner resides	(Child served with copy of petition, represented by guardian *ad litem*)	On such terms as the court thinks proper
SOUTH DAKOTA S. D. COMP. LAWS (1929) §§ 201–211; S. D. Sess. Laws 1937, c. 13; c. 219.	Any adult at least 10 years older than the child. Husband-wife must consent	County court	Parents, mother if child is illegitimate. Child if over 12	"If court satisfied." Name changed
TENNESSEE TENN. CODE ANN. (Williams, 1934) §§ 9561, 9568–9572; Tenn. Acts 1937, c. 310, §§ 1–2.	Any person. Nonresident may adopt if child is placed by or through a Tenn. agency	Circuit, probate or county court in county of petitioner's residence	Agency may be authorized to consent to an adoption by a nonresident	Directs terms, changes name
TEXAS TEX. ANN. REV. CIV. STAT. (Vernon, 1936) art. 46a, §§ 1–10; TEX. ANN.REV.CIV. STAT. (Vernon, 1938) art. 46a, § 6; art. 46b.	Adult resident; husband-wife jointly. No adoption allowed of Negro by white or of white by Negro	District court in district of petitioner's or child's residence	Parents, mother if child is illegitimate; supt. of school or home having custody of child; consent waived if child has been abandoned two years or more. Child if over 14	
UTAH UTAH REV. STAT. ANN. (1933) §§ 14–4–1—14–4–13.	Any adult at least 10 years older than child. Husband or wife must consent	District court in county of petitioner's residence	Parents, mother if child is illegitimate, institution having custody of child. Child if over 12	"If court satisfied." Petitioners execute agreement
VERMONT VT. PUB. LAWS (1933) §§ 3321–3337; Vt. Laws 1937, no. 67, §§ 2–3.	A person of age; husband-wife join or consent	Probate court in district where petitioner resides, or, if nonresident, where child resides	Parents, guardian, selectman, mayor	Form specified

158

SOCIAL ASPECTS
(to 1938)

NOTE: *The provisions here are no less statutory than those on the opposite page but they are essentially social in their meaning. The italics in Column 3 indicate investigation initiated by courts that may or may not have full social welfare emphasis*

3. SOCIAL INVESTIGATION	5. TRIAL PERIOD	7. RECORDS	8. STATUS AND INHERITANCE RIGHTS
			Of adoptee "as lawful child" with restrictions if illegitimate
By probation or other officer of court, or agent of the Division of Child Welfare	Six months	Copy of order sent to Bureau Vital Statistics within ten days	Adopter-adoptee sustain legal parent-child relation. Natural parent, no rights
		Decree entered on minutes, embodies petition	Child has all rights, inherits as heir unless limited by decree. Adopter may not inherit from child
By suitable person selected by court	Six months	Files, records, report of investigation open to inspection or copy only on court order except to parties in interest	Adoptee held to be child of adopter, but with detailed restrictions on inheritance. He may inherit from natural kin but they have no rights. He may will property. Adopter inherits from child
			Child takes family name of adopter with whom he has legal parent-child relationship. Natural parents, no rights
By court which may request information from State's Attorney and others		Instruments filed, recorded by court or by commissioner Public Welfare. Correction of records by town clerk. Certificate of adoption filed with birth record	Adoptee as if the legitimate child of adopter, inherits except property limited to heirs of the body. Natural parents, no rights

STATUTORY ASPECTS
(to 1938)

NOTE: *The legal and social steps by which the petitioner advisedly proceeds toward the adoption of a child are suggested by the numbers heading each column*

STATE	1. PETITION PRESENTED		4. MUST HAVE CONSENT OF	6. DECREE
	BY WHOM?	WHERE?		
VIRGINIA Va. Code Ann. (Michie, 1936) § 5333.	Resident of state; husband-wife jointly	Circuit, corporation, or hustings court in city, or circuit court of petitioner's residence.	Parents, guardian, next friend. Child if over 14	Interlocutory, revocable. Final, sets forth facts, changes name if desired
WASHINGTON Wash. Rev. Stat. Ann. (Remington, 1932) §§ 1696-1699; Wash. Sess. Laws 1935, c. 150, §§ 1-5.	Any inhabitant; husband-wife jointly	Superior court in county of petitioner's residence	Parents, mother if child is illegitimate, guardian, next friend. Child if over 14	"If court satisfied." Sets forth facts, changes name
WEST VIRGINIA W. Va. Code Ann. (Michie, 1937) §§ 4755-4760,4904(81).	Any person at least 15 years older than child. Husband-wife must join or consent	Circuit court in county of petitioner's residence	Parents, guardian, next friend, acknowledged like a deed. Child if over 14	Facts at length. Name changed
WISCONSIN Wis. Stat. (1937) §§ 322.01-322.09, 69.60-69.605.	Adult inhabitant, husband-wife jointly unless one is child's natural parent	County court in county of petitioner's residence	Parents, mother and State Board Control if child is illegitimate; guardian; State Board Control or agency under some circumstances. Child if over 14	Sets forth facts; changes name
WYOMING Wyo. Rev. Stat. Ann. (Courtright, 1931) §§ 20-201—20-216; Wyo. Rev. Stat. Ann. (Courtright, Supp. 1934) §§ 20-217—20-218.	Any suitable person	District court in county where parent resides	Parents, mother if child is illegitimate, guardian, county commissioner, charitable home having custody of child	Decree confirms agreement stating terms

SOCIAL ASPECTS
(to 1938)

NOTE: *The provisions here are no less statutory than those on the opposite page but they are essentially social in their meaning. The italics in Column 3 indicate investigation initiated by courts that may or may not have full social welfare emphasis*

3. SOCIAL INVESTIGATION	5. TRIAL PERIOD	7. RECORDS	8. STATUS AND INHERITANCE RIGHTS
By probation or other court officer or board of public welfare (otherwise similar to Alabama)	One year	Report to Bureau Vital Statistics	Adoptee as child and heir to adopters, his property goes to adoptive kin. Natural parents, no rights
		Detailed records opened only on court order except to parties in interest	Adoptee as child and heir of adopters. Adoptive, not natural kin inherit
		Decree entered in book kept for the purpose	Adoptee as if born to adopters except for some limitations of inheritance. He inherits from natural kin. Afterborn children share with adoptee and they inherit from each other
By court appointing child welfare agency, probation officer, etc.	Six months	Records closed to inspection or copy except to parties in interest or by court order. Names of adopters do not appear. Report to Bureau of Vital Statistics which files original birth registration, issues new certificate that does not reveal illegitimacy.	Adoptee as natural child of adopters except for some limitations of inheritance. Natural parents, no rights
	Six months	Agreement recorded in county recorder's office as evidence of adoption	Child assumes name of adopter with all rights of person and property unless limited by decree

the heads of investigation, trial period, and records, is indicative of the need of more socialization in child welfare laws.

We wish to repeat that the foregoing tabulations are far from complete and are in no sense to be depended upon as infallible or final. Our condensed listings represent a first-hand study of the statutes available to us and were corrected at a number of points from data which we were able to secure through the kindness of the Children's Bureau at Washington.

Present legislation in the parent-child field shows several tendencies: equalization of rights and duties of both parents; socialization of attitude and practice toward the illegitimate child; and increasing control by the state in adoption proceedings with responsibility resting in departments of welfare. Probably the most important recent development in adoption itself is the emphasis now being given to consent, investigation, and trial period. If these trends continue, adoption proceedings will be well safeguarded eventually but complete protection of the adoptive family will be assured only when the rights of inheritance are clarified, especially between the states.

The following documents illustrate some of the types of instruments to be met in the course of adoption proceedings, such as the forms for petition, consent, notice to consenters, interlocutory decree, final decree, and reregistration of birth. In adoption papers, as in all other details, the states differ widely. Here are presented samples of forms now in use, not models.

PETITION FOR ADOPTION [1]

To the Hon.........................Judge of the Orphan's
Court of the County of......................
    Your petitioners, the undersigned, residents of the County of

[1] DEL. REV. CODE (1935) c. 88, sec. 3550

...................., respectfully apply for an order permitting them to adopt as their own child...................,
a minor child aged........years, who is the child of.........
.............and who is now...................

Your petitioners represent that they are financially able and morally fit .to have the care, supervision and training of said child, and desire that the name of said child shall be changed to.............................

....
....
Petitioners.

Address of petitioners:

....
....
....

Address of parents and guardians:

....
....
....

Address of child:

....
....
....

I, the undersigned.....................of the abovementioned child do hereby consent to the adoption prayed for.

....
Mother, Father, Legal Guardian, Next Friend
Witness...............................
Address...............................

To Clerk of the Orphan's Court:

Enter an order of reference to...........................
...................for investigation and report.

....
Judge of Orphan's Court
Witness...............................
Address...............................

CONSENT [2]

Index Number........................
State Board of Charities and Public Welfare

I (we), the undersigned,..........................of the
above mentioned child, do hereby consent to the adoption above
prayed for by..
and..., his wife.

Witnesses:

....
                           Mother

....
                           Father, legal guardian, next friend

                           Address ....

                           ....

The execution of the foregoing consent to the adoption of
...., minor,
by...............and.................., his wife, was this
day duly acknowledged before me by..................and
...........................who are (is) parent (guardian,
custodian) of said..

Witness my hand and seal this........day of........, 19...
My Commission expires: ....
                    Clerk Superior Court or Notary Public

     (SEAL)

                    ....County

ADOPTION NOTICE [3]

A, B, C, D, etc., (names of defendants, if any) and to all
whom it may concern

Take notice that on the..........day of........, A.D. 19..
a petition was filed by....................................
...............in the.............Court of.............
County, for the adoption of a child named..................

[2] N.C. PUB. LAWS (1935) c. 243, sec. 3
[3] ILL. REV. STAT. (Cahill's, 1933) c. 4, ¶2

Now, unless you appear within twenty days after the date of this notice and show cause against such application, the petition shall be taken as confessed and a decree of adoption entered.

Date...............   ....Clerk.
(Date of publication)

INTERLOCUTORY ORDER [4]

Index Number..........................
State Board of Charities and Public Welfare

STATE OF NORTH CAROLINA   IN THE SUPERIOR
COUNTY OF..................   COURT BEFORE THE
   CLERK

In the Matter of the Adoption of

............................,

Minor, by.....................   INTERLOCUTORY
                                       ORDER
and..........................,

His Wife.

Upon an examination and consideration of the report....of the investigating official....assigned to this case and other evidence now available to the Court, it is found by the Court that the home of the petitioner....is a proper and suitable home in which to place the said..
....
and that the adoption of the said..................., minor, by.....................and........................, his wife, is for the best interest of the said child, and the Court hereby tentatively approves the adoption of said child..........
...........by said.....................and............, his wife, and it is further ordered that said minor,.............., be, and he (she) is hereby placed in the care and custody of the petitioner....until further orders of this Court. And it is

[4] N.C. PUB. LAWS (1935) c. 243, sec. 4

expressly ordered that this order shall be provisional only and may be rescinded or modified at any time prior to the final order of adoption which shall be made not less than one year or more than two years after this date. And it is further ordered that until said final order of adoption the said minor shall be and remain a ward of this Court and its care shall be under the supervision of......................Superintendent of Public Welfare of............County (Representative of...........

....

a child-placing agency licensed by the State Board of Charities and Public Welfare), unless otherwise directed by the Court.

This.........day of................, 19.....

....
Clerk Superior Court

...........County, North Carolina.

FINAL DECREE [5]

Index Number.......................
State Board of Charities and Public Welfare

STATE OF NORTH CAROLINA COUNTY OF................:.....	IN THE SUPERIOR COURT BEFORE THE CLERK

In the Matter of the Adoption of

.............................,

Minor, by......................   **FINAL ORDER OF ADOPTION**

and.........................,

His Wife.

The petitioner....in this cause..........................
and .... of ....
...............having filed.........petition on the......
   (Address)

[5] N.C. PUB. LAWS (1935) c. 243, sec. 5

day of................, 19...., praying for the adoption of
................................, a minor, and an interlocutory order having been granted on the......day of........,
19...., placing the said child with petitioner...., and the County
Superintendent of Public Welfare of......................
County (Representative of..............................)

(Child-Placing Agency)

having been designated to keep and maintain supervision over
the said child and examine into the home life and home conditions
and other matters relevant to the said petitioner...., and a satisfactory report having been rendered to the Court; and it appearing
to the Court that the petitioner....are (is) fit and proper person
....to have the care, custody and training of the said child, and
are (is) morally and financially qualified to rear and educate the
said child, it is hereby ordered and declared by the Court that
the relation of parent....and child be established between the
petitioner....and the said child for the life (during the minority)
of the said child. It is further ordered that the name of the said
child be changed from that of..........................
to that of..

This........ day of................, 19.....

....

Clerk Superior Court

............County, North Carolina

(Add Clerk's Certificate on copies for adopting parents and State
Board of Charities and Public Welfare.)

DECREE [6]

STATE OF VERMONT ⎱
............DISTRICT ⎰

Be it remembered, that at............this....day of........
.... 19...., AB of............in the County of........

[6] VERMONT PUB. LAWS (1933) c. 144, sec. 3335

............and State of................, a minor is hereby adopted and made heir at law of CD and EF, husband and wife (or of GH) of...............in the County............and State of................, and said adopted person shall hereafter bear the name of JS.

...............................(LS)

...............................(LS)

...............................(LS)

STATE OF VERMONT ⎫
............DISTRICT ⎰

At...............this...........day of................, 19....appeared CD and EF, (or GH) and AB (or XL, parent, guardian, selectman or mayor) and acknowledged the foregoing instrument by them sealed and subscribed to be their free act and deed.

Before me

JM,   Judge of the........District

REGISTRATION OF LEGAL BIRTH BY ADOPTION [7]

On request of the petitioner or child, after the decree is entered, the Clerk of the Court shall make a certified record, substantially as follows;

CERTIFICATE OF BIRTH

Registration	Registration No.
District...............	.................Court
County Clerk............County................County

Full name of child......................................

Sex of child	Twins or other	Date of Birth
....	....	....

[7] Illinois Laws 1937, pp. 1006–7, secs. 1–8

FATHER   MOTHER

Full Name ....

Residence ....

City ....

County ....

State ....

Docket No......Petition filed.......Decree entered......

I........................Clerk of the...............
Court of.........................County, State of Illinois,
hereby certify that a Decree of Adoption has been entered by the
Honorable..............................Judge of the said
court on the........day of.................A.D.........and
that the said decree contains the facts as above stated by me and
are a true statement of the name of the child by adoption, its
date of birth; the name of the adopting father and mother is
herein made.

....

Clerk of the........................Court of

...........................County, Illinois

SEAL

Stub of form filed as permanent record of the Clerk of the
Court. Separate certificate for each child if more than one is
adopted.

12

The Voice of Research

References have been made throughout this book to various studies which have an important bearing on adoption, and interpretations have been woven into nearly every chapter. Much of the basic source material is of such recent date that little has been published about it except in professional journals and bulletins. Such publications are not always available to the general reader and their language is sometimes so technical as to be hard to interpret. This chapter offers a few simplified digests of varied types of the more significant research. A reading list of research titles will be found in Chapter XIV for those who care to consult the sources.

Naturally one of the most urgent questions by people interested in adoption is: "How do adopted children turn out?" To find some answers, two specialists in child-placing have made somewhat detailed investigations. The pioneer work (*How Foster Children Turn Out* by Sophie van Senden Theis) covered 910 people at least eighteen years old who had been placed by the New York Charities Aid Association. Only 269 of these individuals had been legally adopted, of whom about half were placed under five years of age. As for success in adjustment, fully three fourths of the total number of persons were judged to have met such standards and responsibilities of adult life as self-support, obedience to law, and acceptance of the moral code of the community.

The adopted group had more education than the unadopted, and seemed to have a more successful family relationship. The most significant factor in success seemed to be age at the time of placement, as a large proportion of the most successful were placed under five years. Over one third of the more successful group who had been in their foster homes since early childhood were still living at home, and most of the others, either married or working away from home, maintained contacts with their foster parents. The investigator was impressed with the devotion of the adopters to their children, and with the "courage, loyalty, sense of responsibility, and ambition" of the adopted persons, especially of the 145 foundlings who measured up in every way to the rest of the adopted group.

Another investigation of the results of adoption (*"Fit and Proper"* by Ida R. Parker) covered 852 adoptions in Massachusetts and gave intensive consideration to 100 cases. The insistent lesson from the study is the need of more preplacement investigation. All of the adoptions took place before the Act of 1923 which provided for investigation, and in two thirds of the total number the petition was granted *on the day it was filed in court.* (We have italicized these last words to draw special attention to a practice which, while not completely eliminated in our country today, is so thoroughly disapproved by psychologists, sociologists, and social workers that it lingers only where child welfare is not properly understood.) Little was known of the background of the adoptees. Of eleven to whom mental tests were given after adoption, six were found below normal and several proved unable to make use of the education and travel provided. Several homes were unfit for children. In the special study group of 100, one fourth were still in school; one fourth were supporting themselves and in some instances their adoptive parents. Of the twenty-eight marriages all but three were successful. At least three of the seven persons in correctional institutions were there because of delinquency growing out of the adoption situation. A mutually satisfactory relationship had apparently developed in as many as seventy-one of the families, including two in which children were born subsequent to the adoption. Fully half the ninety-seven living persons had proved themselves "law-abiding, managing their affairs with good sense, and living in accordance with good moral standards," with a further one third giving equal promise. The investigator points out that the group adopted through agencies was relatively much more capable than those taken independently.

Perhaps the most remarkable result of these two studies is the high degree of success and satisfaction in the adoptive relationship in spite of the fact that the placements had occurred practically without the testing and investigation so integrated with good case work today. There is every reason to believe that adoptions made under present safeguards will afford an even greater proportion of success and deeper satisfactions to the adoptive family.

Experimental psychology for several years has been using the adoptive home as a laboratory for studies in the comparative influence of heredity and environment. This type of inquiry is not primarily aimed at adoption, in fact some studies have not differentiated between adopted and other foster children. Such studies are interested mainly in the adoptive home as a fairly controlled family environment for children. By comparing the adopted children with others of the same age and sex living with their own parents, it was thought some approximation could be found of the relative importance of nature and nurture. The studies here described have many implications for adoption, one of the most important being to answer the question: "How much improvement can be expected in a child adopted by people more competent than his natural parents?" This is a pertinent and compelling question since superior homes are desirous of adopting children. In fact the demand exceeds the supply of even fairly promising candidates. It would give many placing agencies a holiday if they could hand over their supply of dull children to the higher quality families on their waiting lists, confident about their somewhat "ugly ducklings" having "swan-like" probabilities. But such questions and problems are not so easily met or solved. There is little in the research so far completed to justify the hope that a plodder will ever be much more than a plodder, though there is ample evidence that he can be led to plod considerably faster.

The psychological studies chosen for description in the next few pages have, for the most part, dealt exclusively with adopted children. The unadopted ones had lived equally long in their foster homes and in other ways the foster relationship corresponded closely with the adoptive. Temporary foster care would not afford the same favorable conditions for development, no matter how good the home, because the security and the emotional satisfaction of the child is so bound up with the feeling of permanence, with the awareness of complete acceptance as a family member.

Among the significant studies is the one made at Stanford University ("The Relative Influence of Nature and Nurture" by Barbara S. Burks). This deals with 214 adopted children between five and fourteen years old, who had been placed in their adoptive homes under the age of twelve months. The majority were illegitimate with relatively unknown backgrounds. Mental tests were given to the children and to their adoptive parents, about whom information was also obtained as to interests, education, income, and other matters. After the adoptive families had been studied they were compared with 105 own families in which the children were of the same age as the adopted children, parents being matched with the adoptive parents in intelligence and occupation. Heredity looms large. The own parents and their children had much more mental resemblance than the adoptive parents and their children. This suggests again the problem of fitting home to child and child to parent in adoptive placement. Books, magazines, and stimulating parental guidance were not enough to push a slow child through high school. There was, however, a *consistent* mental resemblance between adoptive parents and their adopted children. This corroborates what the gardener knows, that the finest soil and climate will not make an American Beauty out of a Rambler rose, but they will bring out larger, earlier, more richly colored ramblers.

An investigation that closely parallels that of Burks was made at the University of Minnesota ("Nature-Nurture and Intelligence" by Alice M. Leahy). The same method was used on 194 adopted illegitimate children placed under six months of age and between five and fourteen years old when the tests were made. They were compared with 194 own children, the two groups carefully matched as to age, sex, parental occupations, and parental schooling. The results of the comparison, like those of Burks, indicated that heredity is the major factor in mental capacity but that environment does consistently play a part.

Some of the rather incidental observations of both Burks and Leahy have almost as much interest for adoption as the more measurable, statistical findings. The favorable environment seemed to improve the social and moral qualities (personality traits) more than the mental ability, which indicates a greater *apparent* mental improvement than was verifiable by tests. This augurs well for afterschool success, particularly of the more able children, since adult functioning is increasingly on the social level, always conditioned, however, on what may be termed the driving power of the mind. Another observation was the loyalty and devotion of the adoptive families which seemed to equal if not to exceed these qualities in the relationship of own parents and children, this in spite of the fact that the likeness intellectually between adoptive parents and children was less than for own parents.

Somewhat in contrast to the Burks and Leahy studies are the two following researches by Freeman and Skeels. The Freeman work was contemporary with Burks's. The Leahy study reported above was stimulated by the divergent findings of Burks and Freeman.

Another study of the same problem but with a somewhat different method ("The Influence of Environment on Intelligence, School Achievement, and Conduct of Foster Children" by Frank N. Freeman and others) was carried out at the University of Chicago. In this instance 401 children who had been in foster homes for at least four years—but all of whom had not been adopted—were tested and the results compared with the average of unselected own children. Over two thirds of the foster children were illegitimate, average age eleven years. In addition to mental tests of both children and parents, information was secured about school and work success, standing in the community, and other pertinent factors.

The average intelligence of the foster children was found to be nearly the same as that of the own children. This was interpreted as showing favorable results from the foster environment since the natural background of the foster children was considerably below the average; that is, the test scores of the foster children were ten to fifteen points higher than would be expected of children coming from such inferior backgrounds as most of them had before placement. The tests were borne out by school achievement since a larger proportion of the foster children were making good in school than was true in the general population. Even more significant was the comparison of children placed under two years of age in better homes with those placed after the age of five in inferior homes, from which it was found that the first group was making more rapid school progress.

In seventy-four cases the tests of the foster children could be compared with their own scores made before placement four or more years previously. The entire group averaged a small gain, with a greater gain for those in the more privileged homes and also a greater gain for those placed at an earlier age. A comparison between brothers and sisters reared in different foster homes showed a greater difference in intelligence than is usually found between brothers and sisters brought up together; and when two unrelated children were reared in the same foster home they were as much alike as brothers and sisters living together, though some of these comparisons were of too small numbers to be statistically conclusive

In spite of variations of technique and differences in the children, the findings of the Burks, Leahy, and Freeman studies agree that an improved home environment will increase the mental capacity a small but consistent amount. However, Freeman tends toward a more environmental interpretation than the others. The limits of ability beyond which improvement cannot be expected are suggested in these studies but these limits, if they are ever revealed, await upon further research.

A long-term study now in progress at the University of Iowa (see Skeels and Skodak studies in our bibliography: "Research Aspects") deals with children placed under six months of age in average and superior adoptive or foster homes. The social, economic, and educational background of the natural parents was much lower than that of the foster parents. The children are being given periodic mental tests and the histories of the natural and foster parents are being evaluated. An interesting feature of this investigation —and one of importance in view of the divergence between the Burks-Leahy position and that of Freeman—is that the Iowa study has grown out of a regular clinical program in connection with routine testing of children on probation for adoption. Probation in Iowa is in accordance with the policy of the Child Welfare Bureau to permit no adoption before the child has been given a psychological examination. When the examiners repeatedly found the test performance higher than would be expected from children with such questionable backgrounds, research was undertaken to look into the influence of environment on the growth of intelligence. As Skodak has pointed out:

Certain broad generalizations emerge from the results of this study. The first is that intelligence is much more responsive to environmental changes than had previously been conceived. Evidence indicates that it is the home rather than the child's true-family background which for practical purposes sets the limits of his mental development. If there is an hereditary constitution which sets the limits of mental development, these limits are extremely broad.

Conclusions drawn thus far from this Iowa series by Skeels and others are: (1) that the average intelligence is higher than would be expected of children coming from the educational, occupational, and socio-economic level of their natural parents; (2) that there is no mental resemblance between the children and their natural mothers so far as coefficient of correlation can reveal; (3) that the mental level of the children compared favorably with children of similar age from families in superior occupational groups; (4) that intelligence is much more responsive to environmental changes than had previously been conceived. (The late Dr. Bird T. Baldwin would be much interested in this outgrowth of his foundation work at Iowa in the 1920's.) A nonstatistical conclusion, but one full of importance for adoption, is that there may be factors, possibly growing out of the adoptive parent-child relationship, that influence mental growth even more than the social and economic condition of the adoptive family. Does the mental stimulation arise in part from the social maturity of the adoptive parents; their readiness, even eagerness, for parenthood which perhaps makes them especially willing to put the child's interests first? This question has emerged before, in a study of opinions and attitudes of adoptive families ("Forty Foster Homes Look at Adoption" by Lee M. Brooks) with the suggestion that by virtue of their deliberately assuming the duties and privileges of parenthood, adopters are likely to be mature, well socialized, and active with regard to preparation and fulfillment of family responsibilities. Will the mental growth aroused by carefully planned play equipment, books, and parental companionship continue at later ages? These questions, particularly the last, may be answered as the Iowa study progresses.

A somewhat related investigation of the effect of environment on intelligence tested children in eight schools of different social status in England ("The Relation Between Intelligence and Social Status Among Orphan Children" by D. C. Jones and A. M. Carr-Saunders). In this case the environment was institutional and the results seem to show a differentiation of intelligence according to social class. The intelligence of the children from the poorer homes increased after they went to live in an orphanage but institutional life had the opposite effect upon the mental powers of children whose homes had been on a higher social level.

In addition to the nature-nurture study mentioned above because of its comparative value, Dr. Leahy has made other extensive studies of the adoptive family. One of these explorations has been selected for brief review here as an example of a sociological type of inquiry. While the investigator herself is the first to admit the limitations of mass characterization, she has, nevertheless, given a valuable composite picture of adoptive parents by means of charts, tables, and statistical formulas. The adoptive parents of

2,414 illegitimate children in Minnesota were the subjects of this investigation ("Some Characteristics of Adoptive Parents" by Alice M. Leahy). It was found that most of these parents were childless couples married nearly ten years before the adoption, with a predominance of city residents. The average school grade reached was the eighth. The proportion of adoptive fathers in professional, business, and managerial occupations greatly exceeded that of adult men in general.

It is clear that psychological and sociological research is making headway in the field of family relations of which adoption is an increasingly important part. Rigorous methods of research applied to humankind do not necessarily mean bloodless conclusions. One of the most careful social scientists has described her study of adoption as "cold research mixed with human heart-beats."

13

Echoes from Adoptive Homes

We have for several years been interested in the attitudes of adoptive parents and adopted children. We have done some exploring to obtain evaluations and expressions of belief from parents and children, but in no sense is our study of sixty families, including sixty-seven adoptees, a cut downward through the general population strata. The parents represent a more selected group, statistically speaking, than those in the studies of the preceding chapter since in˙ our study the participation required not only literacy but powers of analysis and self-expression as well as that most important attribute, a *willingness* to take time to think and write in detail.

These adoptive homes are located in twelve states and Canada, all east of the Mississippi River, twenty-five of them in the North and thirty-five in the South. All the children were taken for adoption under five years of age, one half of them at a year or less. They had been in the adoptive homes from one to twenty-five years at the time the data were gathered; the average experience in adoptive relationship, eight and two-thirds years.

The adopters had held more or less firmly in mind the thought of adoption for varying periods up to ten years, about one half of them for over a year. The age of the mothers at the time of adoption averaged thirty-four years and the fathers, thirty-seven years, or very slightly under the ages for the Minnesota study. The four single mothers were older, averaging forty years.

Occupationally, considerably over one third of the fathers were in business, another one third were in the professions, while a majority of those remaining were farmers. Several of the mothers are or have been in business or professional work.

This study, statistically of slight significance, did not show the usual preponderance of girls. Is it mere chance that in this small group of families the sexes were more evenly divided, or does it point to something unique in the choice of children by the higher occupational and educational groups?

It has been a criticism of adoption as a method of child nurture that the adoptive home is usually the one-child home. In this study eight of the families adopted more than one child, and sixteen other families had own as well as adopted children. Thirty-six children in our study were being brought up as "only" children, and several of their foster parents have testified that more children originally figured in their plans, but that owing to the financial stringency of recent years they have so far been unable to make other adoptions. Some of the younger parents still hope to have another child.

As for the only child situation, recent investigations—far more exacting and conclusive than the study by E. W. Bohannon in 1898—have shown rather clearly that the one-child home is not the menace that so many people have traditionally supposed, if the parents are sufficiently aware of the need of the child for companions of his own age and if they take pains to supply that need. It is likely that the family whose plans included several children will do all in its power to provide compensations when the plans fail of completion. Such homes may be just as successful in socializing the only child as the one where brothers and sisters are found. Certainly, according to clinical researches of problem children, the only child is being given a good score on behavior in place of the traditional tag marked "spoiled."

The larger proportion of families having more than one child may be related to the financial ability of this more selected group. This seems to be borne out by the experience of some of the private placing agencies where well-to-do parents often return for a second, or even a third child.

Affection? The point on which there is greatest agreement among the adoptive parents is that of their love for their chosen children. They are not content with practically unanimous avowal that they could think no more of their child if he were their own flesh and blood, but more than one half of them write fervent and unsolicited testimonials of their affection. Several of those having both own and adopted children say that there is no difference in their feeling toward them. Others speak glowingly of their child's response and appreciation, and a few say that their adopted children are more thoughtful than their own. There is quite general agreement among the parents that the adopted child responds with as much affection and devotion as the own child.

On the question of the child's background there is substantial agreement that a knowledge of it is valuable chiefly as an aid in helping him to make adjustments. There is slight emphasis, in the minds of the adoptive parents, on inherited traits, except that they want their child to be free from mental or physical taint. Several mention specifically that their children came from very poor backgrounds, yet have given satisfaction and have been sources of pride. Only a few parents care to know *all* the details of their child's history and over ninety per cent prefer to be able to say: "I don't know," when questioned closely about it. Similarly, nine tenths of them feel that illegitimacy is not a barrier to adoption. The very few who dislike in general the idea of adopting an illegitimate child admit that this feeling might be overcome by the "right" child.

That the risks of adoption are as great for the child as for the adopters, the parents believe thoroughly and consistently. They seem fully aware that a sound and stable child may be permanently injured by the wrong home.

The motives for adoption in this group are mainly an interest in children, a desire for affectionate response, and an insurance against the insecurity of old age. This last does not necessarily imply financial support, though in some cases that may be a factor, but rather does it refer to security against loneliness, isolation, and other dread aspects common to old age. Almost without exception the parents condemn the exploitive use of children, especially on the farm. Many express themselves forcefully as believing that adoption is justifiable only from motives of helpfulness to the child. Some tell of adopting children in whom they were interested in order to "give them a better chance"; others felt that they were missing one of life's deepest experiences and wished to repair the omission. As might be expected, few purely "selfish" motives are discernible.

Should the child be told of his adoption? Yes, and early. He should grow up with the knowledge. Nearly all parents agree that the main facts should be known before the age of ten. The Theis study showed that at least one third of the adoptive parents had not told their children of their adoption. In at least two thirds of the findings by Burks, the child had never been told of his foster status. The Parker study, without stressing the actual numbers uninformed, does emphasize the great importance of telling the child, and discusses with illustrations the manner in which individuals learned of their adoption: "twitted by her school mates because she was not an own child," a fact hitherto unknown to this ten-year-old; "a bright girl of nineteen unaware of her adoption in spite of the changes" within the family; and other similar instances. However, this study concludes from the information obtained concerning the one hundred individuals that at least three fourths of them were known by persons outside the family to be adopted. The convictions of the expert and the inexpert on this point are so clear as to be overwhelmingly in favor of having the child grow up with the central truth about himself.

Should every discoverable detail be made known to the child? One third of our parents believe he should be spared distressing details, though several are of the opinion that everything should be revealed to him sooner or later. Another third expresses doubt about how much should be disclosed. It seems significant to us that there is such difference of opinion on this point. The parents are speaking out of their own experiences which vary greatly; and many of them are still struggling with this as one of the major issues, hence their doubts. No other subject brought out so much uncertainty, nor so much difference of opinion. It would seem that so far as disclosing intimate detail is concerned, each case must be decided on its merits, in the light of what is known about the child's background and what the community and family attitude may be. It is not always easy to know where to draw the line between disclosure and withholding of detail. Only common sense can decide. Even though no blanket advice can be given, the question must be faced squarely; preparation must be made to deal with it; postponement or evasion is unwise and unsafe.

Taunts of playmates? Some of the parents write of their children being taunted at school, and agree that however they may wish it were unnecessary, the fact of adoption should be told in some form because it will eventually be found out. Some speak of the new security, the increased affection of their children after they were told. Many feel that the knowledge should come in very early childhood long before the dawn of adult-minded comparisons, values, and prejudices. Bit by bit, even as he learns to walk and talk, the idea of his adoption should blend in with other experiences and discoveries of life, very much as sex understanding is a cumulative process. Thus will the child be able to assimilate easily, even to withstand what would otherwise be a jolt, anything that may develop in connection with his adoption. Parents are practically unanimous in believing that the child will not suffer from taunts of playmates if he is secure in the affection of his foster home and if he feels that it has played fair with him.

Community inquisitiveness about adoptions was generally felt to be superficial, mere curiosity, or on the other hand a matter of genuine interest. Harshness of attitude and remark occurred in a very few cases on the part of relatives or friends. Kinfolk and others generally are open-minded, considerate, and even enthusiastic. Most of the parents agreed that the manner in which the child was accepted by the community is dependent upon the reputation of the adopting household, although a few believed that their child had broken down community doubts and prejudices by a winning personality.

Adoption by the unmarried woman is another problem. Parents are not very sure about its advisability. Some of the comments reveal doubts created by a realization of the weight of responsibility that must be borne by the single parent, whether unmarried or widowed. Others point out that the single mother should have an assured income and exceptional health, or that she should have co-operative relatives or friends who would take over the responsibility in the event of her death or disability. Most of the parents think that the unmarried woman should adopt only girls but a few suggest boys as promising greater help and protection. One unmarried woman with an adopted son found that his being the man of the family induced in him attitudes of chivalry and responsibility. Several suggested that the single parent situation needs both the boy and girl element in order to create a more balanced home life for the children as well as the adult, thus to avoid the danger of emotional fixation.

From eighteen adopted persons, most of them now adults themselves, some interesting points in their adoptive experience have come into focus. All but two of them express great appreciation and loyalty to their adoptive parents. Affection has been generously given and thankfully received by all concerned, as much so, they say, as could be true of the own relationship. In fact, it is an expressed source of satisfaction to several sons and daughters that they resemble their adoptive parents. In most cases the association with other children in the family, whether they were own or adopted, was happy. In one household a girl is fond of a younger brother whom she helped to "pick out," but she does not get on well with another brother adopted when she was. Biological siblings do not always agree! There is considerable evidence from the adopted child that adoptive parents have been overindulgent, presumably in an effort to compensate for the child's background.

Nearly all these adoptees have been accepted as blood kin by the relatives of their parents; few have ever suffered in their social contacts by reason of their adoptive status; but two think their adoption or their uncertain past was a factor in broken engagements; and one reports that his wife uses his adoption as her most potent weapon in family disagreements.

Those who have always known of their adoption can remember little if any worry or speculation about it, but several who received the knowledge at a later age confess to shock and sorrow, and one girl resents her adoptive parents' unsuccessful effort to conceal the fact.

Of the two who have not been assimilated happily by their foster homes, one is displeased over the fact or belief that she was a "laboratory" child, that her parents' affection was more intellectual than warmly emotional, that their main interest in her was experimental. The other individual, bordering on mental instability if we judge rightly, feels that she is looked down upon and discriminated against because of her adoption.

In summarizing the contents of this and the preceding chapter, it is scarcely necessary to emphasize the fact that a comparison of research in the field of adoption is difficult because of the wide variation in point of view, in technique, and in findings. The problem is akin to that of all investigations into human affairs. However, the few specific similarities between the researches are all the more significant because of the general differences in approach and methods of study.

The most striking agreement is on the matter of mutual affection and loyalty of the adoptive parents and children, especially in the light of present-day criticisms of family life. In spite of the oft-repeated estimate that family bonds in general are loosening, there is apparently a high degree of satisfaction with the adoptive relationship, sufficient not only to provoke almost extravagant expression on the part of the families concerned, but to attract the notice of field workers and other objective observers.

The composite picture of the adoptive home as we have found it in these sixty cases, is one superior to the average in educational and occupational level, with parents more mature than natural parents, and with a total of from one to three children in the home. The most successful adoptive home seems clearly to be the one where the child was taken into family membership under five years of age, was chosen with the help of a placing agency, was legally adopted after spending a trial period of at least six months in the new home before the final decree was granted, and where the child was told of his adoption at a very early age.

14

On Library Shelves

We have seen how interest in child welfare has increased since the dawn of the twentieth century, with the emphasis first on physical health. Infant mortality has gradually been reduced and many of the more prevalent children's diseases have been brought under control. Attention has also been directed toward mental hygiene aspects and toward social conditions affecting child life. This is strikingly reflected in the writings, popular and scholarly, that have been published since 1920. Still more conspicuous is the increase in publication regarding adoption, particularly in the last decade. A study of the literature indicates a developing public concern in the subject, not alone in the United States but of world-wide extent. Answers to almost any question about adoption can now be found in the various writings that show extreme diversity of style, of viewpoint, and it must be admitted, of accuracy and objectivity. Yet this plenitude of material is not always readily accessible to the general reader nor is he always able to sift the wheat from the chaff. Still less can the professional person and student amid their urgent routines find time to select critically the best material for immediate and practical use. With these and all other busy people in mind we have prepared this list, representative but by no means complete. The titles cover a wide range of articles, books, bulletins, and scientific papers bearing on adoption.

The classification and descriptive notes aim to save the time of the reader, but not to evaluate the writings. On some points where there seems to be general agreement, only a few of many possible titles were chosen; on other points where there is divergence of opinion, care has been taken to balance one extreme with the opposite viewpoint. Some of the bulletins listed are out of print but are still to be found in well-equipped libraries, and are included because no more recent publication quite takes their place.

The first alphabetical grouping covers parent-child aspects of adoption, mostly from run-of-the-home magazines, with a sprinkling of weightier authorship. Here will be found expressions by adoptive parents and adopted children; also publications intended as a guide to adoptive families who have little time for wide reading but who may want a sampling of opinion and fact to direct their thinking.

The second listing has to do with child welfare phases of adoption. Here the content is more substantial with the popular magazines giving way to the journals, bulletins, and books of specialization. It is to be hoped that in this section the student and the professional will find short cuts to a wider viewpoint. It is especially commended to young people who are looking for a research subject or are undecided as to vocational or professional choice. A national leader in child welfare recently gave his opinion that no single subject in this field during the middle 1930's has aroused so much discussion as adoption. The titles listed here may well serve as a starting point for much needed study and action along several fronts.

Higher standards for placement, longer and better supervised probation, uniform state laws and more agreement in interpretation—these are self-evident and immediate needs, and all depend largely on informed public opinion. Courts and welfare workers are, in the main, well aware of the situation but are handicapped not only by oversize dockets and case loads, but also by the constant pressure of adopters and other interested persons who insist that their case is peculiar and should be made the exception. Child welfare specialists the country over urge the need of an educational effort to arouse the public conscience for the protection of both the adopted child and the adopting parents. There is no simpler way to do this than to make accessible to the reading public nontechnical and unsentimental writings on the subject. The social worker, doctor, lawyer, minister, and institutional staff member will find in this second section titles of interest and value. Mr. and Mrs. Average Citizen may also become more sensitive to the problem by such a sampling from the printed page. The authorship is representative, though far from all-inclusive, of leadership in the realms of social work, public welfare, child care, and academic study.

The third grouping goes into the scientific research pertinent to adoption. It is a relatively unexplored field, a challenge to the studious but likely to be a fruitless effort for all who enter it save those with maturity, experience, and access to confidential records of social work and court files. Perhaps the main value of the few titles in this third list is their suggestiveness as to techniques, material, reliability, practical worth, limitations, and so on. Here the purposes and methods aim toward objective measurement in the human field, the scientific spirit focused upon social discovery. The results are not spectacular but they are indicative of the newer objectivity in social science. Human stresses and strains are not reducible to mathematical formulas, human relationships cannot be developed in a test tube, but patience and precision are qualities needed no less by the social scientist than by the physicist or the bacteriologist. Such studies as those cited are a portent that tomorrow's less fortunate children may not be victimized by guess work, sentimentality, and commercial exploitation.

The fourth and last shelf of our library is set apart for legal titles, intended as the merest introductory sampling for orientation in this basic subject. Adoptive parents are sometimes needlessly fearful of the law. As with most writing that uses specialistic vocabularies, at first glance a legal article looks to the layman like a foreign language. Yet most adoption statutes are understandable and have many possibilities of reassurance for the adopter. However, the needs of students and child welfare workers have been chiefly in mind as these titles were selected.

Adoption can be a particularly challenging subject for the student who is grounded in both sociology and law. In other countries doctoral dissertations are being written on adoption, some of which will doubtless furnish the basis for action in programs of improved adoption laws and practice. A study of these works with perhaps translations of the most pertinent, would be a useful addition to our too meagre body of writing on the subject. We need to know what the rest of the world is doing; we need to look objectively at our own peculiar problems in each state; we need to co-ordinate the laws and practices of the different states into a national, or at least a nation-wide program.

It is not too much to say that all students of adoption whether professional or academic, need some legal background, so fundamental is law to adoption. For those to whom it is available an introductory course in Family Law may be the simplest and most satisfactory approach. For others without the facilities of the classroom and able to set their own pace, some understanding of the law as it affects adoption may be gained through reading. The titles in Group IV are offered as a possible starting point, for once a beginning is made the subject leads the student.

Some of the readings in this fourth group as well as those in the second group in Child Welfare Aspects, may prove suggestive and informative to those interested in improving

the laws. Adoption is such a many-sided subject that it
needs scrutiny from many angles before wise legislation can
be enacted. It cannot be seen detached from its legal and
social framework. It cannot be ignored without increasing
confusion in the courts, which inherit our unsolved legislative problems, nor can it be ignored in the interests of child
and family welfare.

In recent years we have been asked many times for the
names of books, bulletins, or articles dealing with this or
that aspect of adoption. Requests have come from adoptive
parents, from would-be adopters, from adopted children,
from teachers, from social workers, from students in search
of an academic project or eager to make some contribution
toward meeting human need. All of these we have in mind
as we present this list which was begun nearly a decade ago
with no thought of publication but in earnest, sometimes
desperate quest for help in our personal problems as an
adoptive family.

Much more remains to be said about adoption; much more
will be said in the years just ahead.

Annotated Bibliography

I. PARENT-CHILD ASPECTS

"Adopted Mother," *Scribners Magazine*, XCVII (January, 1935), 56–59. See also *Readers Digest*, XXVI (February, 1935), 7–10. The mother of one own child and several adopted children argues well for adoption.

"Adopting a Baby," *Woman's Journal*, XIV (July, 1929), 8–10. Offers answers to some of the questions concerning affection, process of adoption, preparation, study period, age of child, and normality.

Adoption. Washington: Children's Bureau, U. S. Dept. of Labor, Folder 13, 1938. 15 pp. The meaning of adoption; what should be known about the child; where can a child be found; the trial period; the state's interest; and other basic considerations simply set forth.

"An Adopted Mother Speaks," *Survey*, XLVII (March, 1922), 962–63. An adoptive mother stresses community attitudes in regard to adoption.

BROMLEY, DOROTHY DUNBAR. "Demand for Babies Outruns the Supply," *New York Times Magazine*, March 3, 1935, p. 9. A feature article on some of the more obvious angles of adoption.

BURKS, BARBARA S. "What Makes Jack a Bright Boy—Home or Heredity?" *North American Review*, CCXXVIII (November, 1929), 599–608. A simplification of nature-nurture research which compared a group of adopted children and their adoptive parents with a group of own children and parents. (See items under III.)

CHAPMAN, A. S. "Homes for Babies; Babies for Homes," *Hygeia*, X (December, 1932), 1106–9. The story of The Cradle, a private placing agency.

CHARTERS, JESSIE A. *Child Training: A Manual for Foster Parents.* Columbus, Ohio: Department of Public Welfare, 1934. 126 pp. This manual gives the fundamentals of child care as shown in the bulletins: "Are You Training Your Child to be Happy?" and "Your Child from One to Six." It is especially adapted to the use of foster and adoptive parents.

CONNOLLY, VERA. "Bargain-Counter Babies," *Pictorial Review*, XXXVIII (March, 1937), 17. A popular article on bootleg adoptions.

CORLEY, HARRIET W. "A Child in the House," *Delineator*, CXIV (January, 1929), 44. A discussion of selected aspects of adoption.

DAVENPORT, CHARLES B. "Child Development from the Standpoint of Genetics," *Scientific Monthly*, XXXIX (August, 1934), 97–116. A statement of the principles of biological heritage.

"Doctors and Infant Adoptions," *Northwest Medicine*, XXXII (November, 1933), 479–80. Points to some of the unfortunate situations that may arise when an infant is hastily placed by the physician attending its birth.

193

DRAWBELL, JAMES W. *Experiment in Adoption.* Toronto: Ryerson Press, 1935. 175 pp. A popular account of the reactions of the author's two-year-old daughter to a baby adopted at ten months.

FRAZER, ELIZABETH. "The Baby Market," *Saturday Evening Post,* CCII (February 1, 1930), 25. A journalistic approach to adoption with babies as the market and childless families as the investors.

GAGLIARDO, RUTH G. "We Wanted Children," *Parents Magazine,* XII (May, 1937), 28–29. Confessions from an adoptive mother of three; indicates some of the difficulties and rewards of adoption in a teacher's family.

GALLAGHER, ELEANOR G. *The Adopted Child.* New York: Reynal and Hitchcock, 1936. 291 pp. A book intended for adoptive parents and social workers covering such points as procedure for adopters, reasons for adopting, heredity versus environment, skepticism of mental tests, telling the child of his adoption, heavy emphasis upon illegitimacy, adoption nurseries.

GIBSON, MRS. CHARLES D. "When a Child Adopts You," *Good Housekeeping,* LXXXV (July, 1927), 79. Some of the "risks of adoption" are compared with the risks of childless homes.

HANNA, AGNES K. "Adoption," *Social Welfare Bulletin,* VII (November-December, 1936), 1–4, 10. Two radio talks on procedure and problems of adoption.

HARRINGTON, JOSEPH. "Orphans: Prisoners of Charity?" *Reader's Digest,* XXX (June, 1937), 45–48, condensed from *McCalls Magazine,* (April, 1937) under title, "Orphans Lost to Love." Makes a point about crowded institutions and relatively few adoptions. (See Worthington article below.)

JENKINS, R. L. "On Adopting a Baby," *Hygeia,* XIII (December, 1935), 1066–68. A few rules for prospective adopters.

LANMAN, ANNE. "Foster Parents Speak for Themselves," *Child Welfare League of America Bulletin,* IX (April, 1930), 4. Mainly the story told by one adoptive father at a round-table discussion.

LEVINSON, A. "When Adopting a Baby," *Hygeia,* VII (February, 1929), 135–38. Some warnings for adopting parents.

LOCKRIDGE, FRANCES. "How to Adopt a Child," *Children* (now *Parents Magazine*), III (October, 1928), 14–15. Also in pamphlet form, 22 pages. Answers questions, doubts, and fears of adopting parents; outlines procedure for adopting, and lists some reliable agencies.

MACKAYE, MILTON. "The Cradle," *Saturday Evening Post,* CCX (April 9, 1938), 12–13. Describes an adoption nursery in Chicago, its individualistic methods, etc.

"My Half Million Dollars," *Forum,* XCVIII (July, 1937), 33–37. A man writes of his will providing a $500,000 subsidy for adoptions in his home city.

NELSON, JOSEPHINE. "Would You 'Bootleg' a Baby?" *Independent Woman,* XV (February, 1936), 42–44. The single woman; should she adopt a child? Factors to be considered are male relatives, family willingness to care for child in event of her death, avoidance of emotional dependence.

NORRIS, KATHLEEN. "Adopt That Baby," *Ladies Home Journal,* XLVII (April, 1930), 8. A well-known author cites her own experience in adoption.

PERKINS, H. F. "Adoption and Fertility," *Eugenical News*, XXI (1936), 95–101. Discussion of birth of children, to previously barren couples, after adoption; 200 out of 273 cases.

POPENOE, PAUL. "The Foster Child," *Scientific Monthly*, XXVIII (September, 1929), 243–48. Warnings from a biologist concerning heredity of candidates for adoption.

——*Practical Applications of Heredity*. Baltimore: Williams and Wilkins, 1930. 122 pp. Chapter VII on "Selecting a Child for Adoption" points out some biological considerations for the adopting parent.

RICKS, JAMES H. *Legal Aspects of Adoption*. New York: Child Welfare League of America, mimeographed bulletin, 1937. 13 pp. An address packed with information by a Virginia judge.

SARGENT, H. D. "Is it Safe to Adopt a Child?" *Parents' Magazine*, X (October, 1935), 26. An unusual view of the problem: Are adoptive parents safe for their children?

SAYLES, MARY B. *Substitute Parents*. New York: Commonwealth Fund, 1936. 309 pp. A study of foster families; a psychiatric approach for and about foster parents both boarding and adoptive, with case stories that illustrate some of the problems in foster care of children.

TAFT, JESSIE. "What It Means to Be a Foster Parent," *Progressive Education*, III (October, 1926), 350–54. Implications for the adopting parent in the change of emphasis from the biological to the social aspects of parenthood.

——"Concerning Adopted Children," *Child Study*, VI (January, 1929), 85–87. The author contends for personal security for the parent in order to avoid projecting his uncertainties upon the adopted child.

TURNBULL, AGNES S. "The Great Adventure of Adopting a Baby," *American Magazine*, CVII (May, 1929), 44. An adoptive mother tells some of her experiences and presents the question: "Are we going to turn out well as parents?"

VANSANT, MARTHA. "The Life of the Adopted Child," *American Mercury*, XXVIII (February, 1933), 214–22. An adopted child tells how wrong emotional attitudes of adoptive parents may warp the lives of their children.

WILLSIE, HONORÉ. "The Adopted Mother," *Century Magazine*, CIV (September, 1922), 654–68. An adoptive mother discloses some of her feelings and experiences.

WORTHINGTON, WILLIAM. "Why Can't We Have an Orphan?" *Survey*, LXXIII (November, 1937), 362. A child welfare worker explains why only a small proportion of children in institutions are adoptable. (Compare with Harrington article above.)

II. CHILD WELFARE ASPECTS

ABBOTT, GRACE. "Adoption," *Encyclopaedia of the Social Sciences*, I (1930), 460–63. A brief historical account with discussion of the present status of adoption.

——*Social Service Review*, XI (September, 1937), 552–54. A review of the Report of the Departmental Committee on Adoption Societies and Agen-

cies, a committee appointed to investigate adoption practices in England
ten years after the passing of the Adoption Act.

——*The Child and the State.* 2 vols.   Chicago: University of Chicago Press,
1938.   Vol. II, 669 pp.   Section III, Adoption, pages 164–228, briefly
summarizes adoption legislation from the social viewpoint, with some
suggestions for improvement, and outlines the present status of adoption
in the United States and Europe.   Several adoption statutes are quoted,
together with public welfare reports.   Sections I and II, The Development of Public Care for Dependent Children, and Interstate Placement
of Dependent Children, together with Part III, The State and the Child
of Unmarried Parents, are also pertinent to adoption.

BAYLOR, EDITH M. H.   "Establishing Foster Parental Relationships," *National
Conference of Social Work Proceedings* 1929, pp. 137–39.   A short summary
of the role of the social worker in establishing foster relationships.

BAYLOR, EDITH M. H. and MONACHESI, ELIO D.   *The Rehabilitation of
Children.*   New York: Harper, 1939. 560 pp.   Pages 29–35 discuss some
of the central aims and hazards in contemporary adoption; pages 310–67,
detailed statistical treatment of the foster home; pages 21–29, discussion
of the unmarried mother of secondary importance in connection with
adoption.

BONAPART, JOSEPH.   "Sociology and the Care of Dependent Children,"
Social Forces, XII (May, 1934), 515–22.   A sociological interpretation
of foster home and institutional care.

BRECKINRIDGE, S. P.   *The Family and the State.*   Chicago: University of
Chicago Press, 1934.   557 pp.   Section VII on adoption, pages 356–414,
gives a survey and interpretation of adoption laws in the United States
and a discussion of the status of adoption in England.

BROOKS, LEE M.   "Forty Foster Homes Look at Adoption," *Family,* XV
(March, 1934), 13–17.   A simplification of a study of attitudes and
opinions given by adoptive parents.

BROOKS, EVELYN C. and BROOKS, LEE M.   "Some Scientific and Professional
Views of Adoption," *Social Forces,* XVII (May, 1939), 509–13.   Lists
seventy-five representative titles of research and professional interest
published since 1924; introductory discussion.

BURGESS, ERNEST W.   "Family Tradition and Personality Development,"
National Conference of Social Work Proceedings 1928, pp. 322–30.   A
sociological interpretation of nature-nurture studies of adopted children.

CHAPIN, H. D.   "Babies Wanted," *Review of Reviews,* VIII (August, 1928),
183–85.   A physician summarizes the history of adoption and advocates
it under proper safeguards as a means of care for dependent children.

Children Indentured by the Wisconsin State Public School.   Washington:
Children's Bureau, U. S. Dept. of Labor, Pub. No. 150, 1925. 132 pp.
Contains a record study of adopted children having child welfare im-
plications in the field of placement.

Child Welfare Bibliography.   New York: Child Welfare League of America,
1937. 32 pp.

CLOTHIER, FLORENCE.   "The Problems of Frequent Replacement of the
Young Dependent Child," *Mental Hygiene,* XXI (October, 1937), 549–58.
Points out dangers to the developing personality of a child subjected to

frequent temporary placement, such as retardation of emotional development, disregard of social values and responsibilities.

COLBY, MARY R. "Responsibility of the State in Child Adoption," *The Child*, II (March-April, 1938), 194–98. Blends social and legal aspects of adoption, with a plea for co-operation of courts and social agencies toward more investigation and better placement.

COLE, LAWRENCE C. "A Study of Adoptions in Cuyahoga County," *Family*, VI (January, 1926), 259–64. A summary of Ohio adoption laws and the results of a study of a year's adoptions in the county of which Cleveland is a part.

——"The Private Children's Agency—Its Possibilities and Limitations," *Family*, XVIII (May, 1937), 80–85. Suggests a workable division of labor for the public and private agencies in adoption work.

COWAN, EDWINA A. "Some Emotional Problems Besetting the Lives of Foster Children," *Mental Hygiene*, XXII (July, 1938), 454–58. A look at the main sources of difficulty in adjustment; points to the break in continuity between the child's past and present situation, and suggests the need of education for foster parenthood.

CRUTCHER, H. B. "Some Misplaced Children," *Survey*, LVI (April 15, 1926), 83–84. Cases found by the Minneapolis Child Guidance Clinic pointing to the need of careful placement.

DEARDORFF, NEVA R. "The Welfare of Said Child," *Survey*, LIII (January 15, 1925), 457–60. An account of the findings of the Children's Commission of Pennsylvania regarding adoption laws and practices in that state.

DE WEERDT, ESTHER H. *Five Years of Child Welfare under the Children's Code in Wisconsin, 1929–1934*. Madison: Wisconsin Conference of Social Work. 148 pp. The report of a study made to find how the Children's Code was working in Wisconsin. Chapter IV deals with child placement, adoptions, illegitimacy, and has implications for any state.

DOWLING, ANNA. "Safeguarding Children and Foster Parents in Adoption Proceedings," *Proceedings of Eighteenth National Conference Catholic Charities*, 1933, pp. 109–15. A round-table discussion.

DUREA, M. A. "Child Placement," *Welfare Magazine*, XVIII (1927), 1182–86. Suggestions as to the contributions of clinical psychology to placement of children in foster homes.

FEARING, ALDEN. "A Home and a Chance in Life," *World's Work*, XXVIII (June, 1914), 192–97. The author balances the foster home against the institution with a good word for both.

Foster-Home Care for Dependent Children. Washington: Children's Bureau, U. S. Dept. of Labor, Pub. No. 136, 1926. 289 pp. This bulletin contains contributions by a dozen leaders in child welfare; much emphasis is given to child placing; appendices dealing with historic, domestic, and foreign customs and laws relating to foster home care.

FRASER, GLADYS G. *Licensing of Boarding Homes, Maternity Homes, and Child Welfare Agencies*. Chicago: University of Chicago Press Social Service Monograph, 1937. 107 pp. A monograph based on legislative and administrative procedures in effect in 1935.

FREEMAN, FRANK N. "An Investigation of the Intelligence of Foster Children," *Social Service Review*, III (March, 1929), 30–34. The results of a study of 401 foster children to discover the effect of favorable home environment on their intelligence and achievement.

GESELL, ARNOLD. *Psychoclinical Guidance in Child Adoption.* Washington: Children's Bureau, U. S. Dept. of Labor, 1926. 12 pp. (Section added to *Foster Home Care for Dependent Children,* Publication No. 136.) A physician-psychologist considers some of the risks of adopting a child with inferior mental capacity, and how to reduce such risks by psychological testing.

——"Reducing the Risks of Child Adoption," *Child Welfare League of America Bulletin,* n.s., VI (May 15, 1927), 1–2. Similar in content to the government publication listed just above.

HANNA, AGNES K. "Some Problems of Adoption," *The Child,* I (December, 1936), 3–7. A discussion of the roles of legislation and social work in adoption, and a description of the Children's Bureau study of adoption in seven states.

——"Interrelationship between Illegitimacy and Adoption," *Child Welfare League of America Bulletin,* XVI (1937), 1. Presents the findings of a Children's Bureau study in nine states.

HASTINGS, RUTH. *The Nationality of Children.* Washington: National League of Women Voters, mimeographed bulletin, January, 1933. 15 pp. Includes notes on nationality of adopted children and the general problem of dual nationality.

HEISTERMAN, C. A. "Summary of Legislation on Adoption," *Social Service Review,* IX (June, 1935), 269–93. An analysis of state laws with emphasis on protective features.

——*Summary of Legislation on Adoption.* Washington: Children's Bureau, U. S. Dept. of Labor, mimeographed bulletin, 1935. 38 pp. An analysis of state laws under such headings as Social Investigation; Trial Period; Consent; Transfer of Custody; Effect of Adoption; Annulment; Interstate Adoption; Records and Reports; Jurisdiction.

HEWINS, KATHARINE P. and WEBSTER, L. J. *The Work of Child-Placing Agencies.* Washington: Children's Bureau, U. S. Dept. of Labor, Pub. No. 171, 1927. 223 pp. A descriptive study of ten agencies caring for dependent children in four areas of the United States. Adoption policy, pp. 78–82.

Historical Summary of State Services for Children in Ohio. Washington: Children's Bureau, U. S. Dept. of Labor, Pub. No. 239, Part 1, 1937. A bulletin intended for students of public welfare administration on the development of Ohio services for children.

JENKINS, R. L. "Adoption Practices and the Physician," *Journal American Medical Association,* CIII (August 11, 1934), 403–8. Notes on qualifications for the adoptive home and for the adopted child from the physician's viewpoint.

JONES, ELIZABETH N. "The Administration of the Adoption Law in Cook County, Illinois," *Social Service Review,* XI (December, 1937), 665–92. An evaluation of the status of adoption in Illinois both as to law and administration.

KENDALL, EVANGELINE. *List of References on Illegitimacy.* Washington: Children's Bureau, U. S. Dept. of Labor, mimeographed bulletin, December, 1935. 7 pp.

"The Least of These," *Child Welfare League of America Bulletin,* VIII (September, 1929), 1. Comments on newspaper advertisements concerning children for adoption.

LIPPMAN, H. S. "Suitability of the Child for Adoption," *American Journal of Orthopsychiatry,* VII (1937), 270–73. Report of an inquiry to determine how those engaged in mental hygiene deal with adoption.

List of References on Adoption. Washington: Children's Bureau, U. S. Dept. of Labor, mimeographed bulletin, March, 1937. 8 pp.

LUNDBERG, EMMA O. and LENROOT, KATHARINE F. *Illegitimacy as a Child Welfare Problem.* Washington: Children's Bureau, U. S. Dept. of Labor, Pub. No. 66, Part 1, 1920. 105 pp.; Pub. No. 75, Part 2, 1921. 408 pp. A report of an investigation of the illegitimate child as a community or public problem, with references to and implications for adoption.

MANGOLD, G. B. *Children Born out of Wedlock.* University of Missouri Social Science Series, III, No. 2, 1921. 209 pp. A sociological study of illegitimacy with scattering references to adoption.

MURPHY, J. PRENTICE. "Foster Care of Neglected and Dependent Children," *Annals American Academy Political and Social Science,* LXXVII (May, 1918), 117–30. An expert in child welfare summarizes the essentials of case work for dependent children, with some emphasis on adoption.

——"Adoption—a Perennial Topic," *Child Welfare League of America Bulletin,* VIII (March, 1929), 2. Stresses the need for more investigation and better records.

MYERS, EARL D. "The English Adoption Law," *Social Service Review,* IV (March, 1930), 53–63. A critical summary of the English Adoption Act of 1926.

"Newspapers Co-operate in Adoptions," *Child Welfare League of America Bulletin,* n.s., VI (January 15, 1927), 1. Instances of newspaper co-operation in discouraging advertisements of children for adoption.

NIMS, ELINOR. "Experiments in Adoption Legislation," *Social Service Review,* I (June, 1928), 241–48. This article, based on a monograph treating adoption in Illinois, deals with adoption legislation in the United States and in England, and proposes further enactments.

——*The Illinois Adoption Law and Its Administration.* Chicago: University of Chicago Press Social Service Monograph No. 2, 1928. 127 pp. A summary of experiments in adoption legislation and the story of the development of the adoption law in Illinois.

OTTO, MARGARET M. *Foster Family Care.* New York: Russell Sage Foundation Bulletin, No. 139, 1936. 4 pp. A selected bibliography.

PAGET, BLANCHE J. *The A-B-C of Foster Family Care for Children.* Washington: Children's Bureau, U. S. Dept. of Labor, Pub. No. 216, 1933. 50 pp. A handbook for those engaged in placing children in foster homes. Pages 34–38: "Wanted, A Child to Adopt" deals with placement for adoption.

PARKER, F. B. "A Study of the Social Adjustment of the Adopted Child." Unpublished thesis University of North Carolina, 1935. 98 pp. General study and special analysis of ten cases suggest that adoption has little importance in determining social status; aside from a few hazards, the adopted child's social adjustments are like those of the own child.

PARKER, IDA R. "Interdependence of Doctor and Social Worker in Legal Adoption," *New England Journal of Medicine,* CC (April 26, 1929), 883–86. A summary of a study of adoptions in Massachusetts with a discussion of legal and social aspects emphasizing need for greater co-operation between doctors, lawyers, and social workers.

——"Adoption," *Social Work Year Book,* I (1929), 23–25; II (1933), 23–25. A brief discussion of legal and social factors.

PECK, EMELYN F. *Adoption Laws in the United States.* Washington: Children's Bureau, U. S. Dept. of Labor, Pub. No. 148, 1925. 51 pp. A summary of the development of adoption legislation and significant features of adoption statutes with text of selected laws.

PENDLETON, ORA. "New Aims in Adoptions," *Annals American Academy Political and Social Science,* CLI (September, 1930), 154–61. Shows the need for study, care, and skill on the part of all concerned including the social worker.

——"Adoption," *Social Work Year Book,* III (1935), 23–25. A brief discussion of legal and social factors.

——"Agency Responsibility in Adoption," *The Family,* XIX (April, 1938), 35–42. An experienced child welfare worker explains the philosophy of case work as it affects placement and summarizes agency responsibility to the child, his natural parents, and the adopting parents.

The Placing of Children in Families. 2 vols. Geneva: League of Nations, 1938. Vol. I, 154 pp.; Vol. II, 241 pp. (Columbia University Press, International Documents Service.) These volumes deal with basic concepts, development, differing systems, principles and procedures throughout the world under national headings; emphasis on foster placement.

"Registration of Births of Illegitimate and Adopted Children," *American Journal Public Health* (Supplement), XXIV (February, 1934), 84–87. Final comments and recommendations of a committee appointed by the Vital Statistics Section of the American Public Health Association.

RICHMAN, LEON H. "Educating Foster Parents," *Jewish Social Service Quarterly,* VII (June, 1931), 32–35. A description of the work of the Jewish Home Finding Society of Chicago in training prospective foster parents for child care.

ROSS, MARY. "Children Who Had a Second Chance," *Survey,* LII (July 1, 1924), 382–85. A review of *How Foster Children Turn Out* by Sophie van Senden Theis, mentioned here because the original publication is out of print and somewhat difficult to obtain. (See III listing research publications and also Theis annotation below.)

SLINGERLAND, W. H. *Child Placing in Families.* New York: Russell Sage Foundation, 1919. 261 pp. A text that combines theory and practice, primarily for students and welfare workers. It gives a broad, general view with emphasis on case work. Adoption is dealt with mainly from the standpoints of selection of children and of legal aspects.

STONEMAN, A. H. "Safeguarding Adoptions, Legally and Socially," *National Conference of Social Work Proceedings,* 1924, pp. 144–50. A plea for more scientific study and less sentiment in child placing.

SYMMES, EDITH F. "An Infant-Testing Service as an Integral Part of a Child Guidance Clinic," *American Journal Orthopsychiatry,* III (October,

1933), 409–30. Shows how such service can aid in safeguarding adoptions.

TARACHOW, SIDNEY. "Disclosure of Foster-Parentage to a Boy," *American Journal of Psychiatry*, XCIV (September, 1937), 401–12. Discusses behavior problems and other psychological results of disclosure of foster parentage, illustrated by seven case histories of boys in the New York State Training School.

TAYLOR, H. B. *Law of Guardian and Ward.* Chicago: University of Chicago Press Social Service Monograph, No. 35, 1935. 194 pp. History of pertinent law, summary of present statutes, suggestion for uniform legislation.

THEIS, SOPHIE VAN S. and GOODRICH, CONSTANCE. *The Child in the Foster Home.* New York: New York School of Social Work, 1921. 150 pp. Gives principles and methods in selection of children and of homes; includes adoption procedure.

THEIS, SOPHIE VAN S. "How Foster Children Turn Out," *National Conference of Social Work Proceedings*, 1928, pp. 121–24. A brief digest of a statistical study of 910 foster children. (See III, Research listing.)

——"Adoption," *Social Work Year Book*, IV (1937), 23–25. Discusses the present status of adoption in the United States; nature and size of the problem, legislation, significance of adoption, agency aids, standards, and studies.

——*Social Aspects of Child Adoption.* New York: Child Welfare League of America, mimeographed bulletin, 1937. 9 pp. An address made before a League conference with stress upon the need and the value of the social agency as an aid to adoption.

THURSTON, HENRY W. *The Dependent Child.* New York: New York School of Social Work, 1930. 337 pp. An historic account of changing aims and methods in the care of the dependent child from the days of feudalism to the present. Adoption is discussed from several angles.

TOWLE, CHARLOTTE. "Evaluation of Homes in Preparation for Child Placement," *Mental Hygiene*, XI (July, 1927), 460–81. A home-finding supervisor discusses the emotional and other elements in child placing.

——"How to Know a Foster Family," *Child Welfare League of America Bulletin*, VII (April 15, 1928), 2–3, and (May 15, 1928), 2–3. An appraisal of prospective foster homes with emotional balance indicated as the most important requisite.

——"Evaluation and Management of Marital Situation in Foster Homes," *American Journal Orthopsychiatry*, I (April, 1931), 271–83. A problem child? Find the problem parent. Problem parent? Look for marital unadjustment.

WAITE, EDWARD F. "Placement of the Child Born out of Wedlock," *Child Welfare League of America Bulletin*, XI (December, 1932), 2–3. A Minnesota judge tells of his state's legal protection of the illegitimate child which effort at safeguarding, nevertheless, does not entirely prevent baby bootlegging and other backdoor methods.

WALKER, GEORGE. *The Traffic in Babies.* Baltimore, Maryland Vice Commission, 1918. 156 pp. The report of a three-year investigation of the disposition of unwanted babies.

WEBSTER, L. JOSEPHINE. "Foster Children and the Changing I.Q.," *Family*,

XII (December, 1931), 257–61. An experienced child welfare worker discusses mental and social factors in adoption.

WHITTON, CHARLOTTE. "Geneva Standards in Child Placing," *The Child,* III (July, 1938), 6–9. Summary of conclusions drawn from the report of 42 countries on the history, philosophy, and fundamental principles of child placing.

WILLIAMSON, MARGARETTA A. *The Social Worker in Child Care and Protection.* New York: Harper, 1931. 485 pp. Duties, responsibilities, relationships, qualifications, and conditions of work are described; job analyses of positions in various types of child caring agencies including those making placements for adoption.

ZACHRY, CAROLINE B. *Personality Adjustments of School Children.* New York: Scribners, 1929. 306 pp. This contains in Chapter IV, pp. 184–212, a case study of an overdependent adopted child; an example of "social heritage." The child, adopted in infancy, acquired traits of the adoptive family, especially those of the mother.

III. RESEARCH ASPECTS

BURKS, BARBARA S. "Relative Influence of Nature and Nurture upon Mental Development," *Year Book National Society for Study of Education,* XXVII (1928), Part 1, Chapter X, 219–316. A comparative study of a group of foster children and a group of true or "own" children.

——"Comments on Chicago and Stanford Studies of Foster Children," *Year Book National Society for Study of Education,* XXVII (1928), Part 1, Chapter XI, 317–22. Brief statement of points of agreement and of difference between these two studies.

EPSTEIN, RUTH and WITMER, HELEN. "Some Suggestions for Illinois Adoption Procedure," *Smith College Studies in Social Work,* VIII (June, 1938), 369–388. A study of sixty adopted children who showed behavior difficulties, nearly half of which developed out of the adoption situation.

FREEMAN, FRANK N. and others. "Influence of Environment on Intelligence, School Achievement, and Conduct of Foster Children," *Year Book National Society for Study of Education,* XXVII (1928), Part 1, Chapter IX, 103–217. Comparative tests of a group of children before placement and after several years of residence in foster homes. A brief summary may be found in *Social Service Review,* III (March, 1929), 30–34.

FREEMAN, FRANK N. "Heredity and Environment in the Light of the Study of Twins," *Scientific Monthly,* XLIV (January, 1937), 13–19. Report of a Chicago University study of nineteen pairs of identical twins separated in infancy compared with twins reared together; has implications for adoption.

JONES, M. C. and BURKS, BARBARA S. *Personality Development in Childhood.* (Monograph Social Research in Child Development, I, No. 4), 1936. 205 pp. A survey of problems, methods, and experimental findings. Part 2 deals with hereditary tendencies, cultural influences, intelligence and physical factors in relation to personality traits; has implications for adoption.

JONES, D. C. and CARR-SAUNDERS, A. M. "Relation Between Intelligence and Social Status Among Orphan Children," *British Journal Psychology*

(Genetic Section), XVII (1927), 343–64. Comparative tests of orphans from eight schools of different social status.

LEAHY, ALICE M. "A Study of Certain Selective Factors Influencing Prediction of the Mental Status of Adopted Children," *Pedagogical Seminary and Journal of Genetic Psychology*, XLI (December, 1932), 294–329. Comparative study of adopted illegitimate children and illegitimate children retained by their true mothers to observe resemblance of mentality.

——"Some Characteristics of Adoptive Parents," *American Journal Sociology*, XXXVIII (January, 1933), 548–63. A sociological study of adoptive parents of illegitimate children.

——"Nature-Nurture and Intelligence," *Genetic Psychology Monographs*, XVII (1935), 235–308. Comparative study of a group of adopted illegitimate children and a group of children living with their true, legitimate parents.

——"A Study of Adopted Children as a Method of Investigating Nature-Nurture," *Journal American Statistical Association*, XXX (March, 1935), 281–87. An investigation of the influence of selective placement in discovered resemblance between intelligence of adopted children and that of their adoptive parents.

——*The Measurement of Urban Home Environment*. Minneapolis: University of Minnesota Press, 1936. 70 pp. Description of a rating scale for measuring homes for such purposes as child placement.

MURPHY, J. F. *The Dependent Boy*. Washington: Catholic University of America, 1937. 204 pp. A comparative analysis of three groups of boys living in institutions, in foster homes, and in their own homes.

PARKER, IDA R. *"Fit and Proper?"* Boston: Distributed by the Church Home Society, (published by the Research Bureau on Social Case Work), 1927. 130 pp. A statistical study of 852 adoptions in Massachusetts, with critical analysis of 100 cases.

RECKLESS, WALTER C. "A Sociological Case Study of a Foster Child," *Journal of Educational Sociology*, II (June, 1929), 567–84. This suggests a technique for studying relationships of a child four to eight years old. By observing him in his contacts with children and adults, insight will be gained that will make for his proper placement.

SCHOTT, E. L. "I. Q. Changes in Foster Home Children," *Journal of Applied Psychology*, XXI (1937), 107–12. Clinical examination of 200 children, 18 months to 17 years old before placement, 1929–1934, followed by a retest of 74 children. The gain after placement is statistically insignificant.

SHEA, ALICE LEAHY. "Family Background and Placement of Illegitimate Children," *American Journal Sociology*, XLIII (1937), 103–4. A record study of adopted illegitimate children in Minnesota.

SHUTTLEWORTH, F. K. "The Nature versus Nurture Problem," *Journal Educational Psychology*, XXVI (1935), 561–78 and 655–81. Definition of the problem with a statistical analysis in terms of variance attributable to heredity, to environment, and to heredity-environment; implications for further research.

SKEELS, H. M. "Relation of Foster Home Environment to Mental Development of Children Placed in Infancy," *Child Development*, VII (March, 1936), 1–5. A statistical study in Iowa of 73 children placed in foster homes when under six months of age to compare their intelligence with that of their true and foster parents.

——"Mental Development of Children in Foster Homes," *Pedagogical Seminary and Journal Genetic Psychology*, XLIX (1936), 91–106. The first unit of a long-time study of mental development of children placed in infancy in foster homes superior to their natural homes.

——"Mental Development of Children in Foster Homes," *Journal of Consulting Psychology*, II (1938), 33–43. Results of a study of 147 children placed in foster homes when under six months of age.

SKODAK, MARIE. *Children in Foster Homes: A Study of Mental Development*. University of Iowa Studies in Child Welfare, Vol. XVI, No. 1. Iowa City: State University of Iowa, 1939. 155 pp. Follows Skeels' study; about two groups of orphan children, total 219, placed in foster homes. Evidence shows the foster home as influencing the I.Q. upward despite true parental background. "If there is an hereditary constitution which sets the limits of mental development, these limits are extremely broad."

THEIS, SOPHIE VAN SENDEN. *How Foster Children Turn Out*. New York: State Charities Aid Association, No. 165, 1924. 239 pp. A statistical study of 910 foster children, many of them legally adopted. Emphasis is on family background, the value of the foster relationship, response of child to educational opportunity, work, standards of conduct, and place in the community. Main conclusion: the most successful subjects were placed at an early age and legally adopted.

IV. LEGAL ASPECTS

BOOKS

1 *American Jurisprudence* (1936) 619–677. (This legal encyclopaedia covers all legal phases of adoption and gives a compact general picture.)

2 *Corpus Juris Secundum* (1936) 365–460. (This is another reference book which describes the history and present status of adoption from the legal viewpoint.)

MADDEN, *Handbook of the Law of Persons and Domestic Relations* (1931) 354–368. (The section on "Adoption of Children" is a brief textbook discussion of such points as qualifications, consent, domicile, jurisdictions, status, inheritance, and revocation.)

STUMBERG, *Principles of Conflict of Laws* (1937) 307–310. (Chapter X, "Adoption," is a brief textbook discussion of conflicting laws concerning adoption, covering such points as jurisdiction, procedure, and inheritance.)

4 VERNIER, *American Family Laws* (1936) 279–549; (Supp. 1938) 118–132. (The sections on adoption comprise both reference material and interpretative comments, with suggestions for legislative needs. The statutes are both summarized and arranged in tabular form. Under each heading is a selected list of references including books, articles, case notes, and other valuable leads for further study.)

ARTICLES AND NOTES

ARMOUR, *The Legitimation and Adoption Act* (1927) 5 CAN. B. REV. 189. (A criticism of the Canadian Legitimation and Adoption Act of 1921 to the effect that the language is equivocal.)

BROSNAN, *The Law of Adoption* (1922) 22 COL. L. REV. 332. (A brief historic survey which points out features of Roman and pre-Roman as well as continental European and English law, with an argument for uniform laws in the United States.)

CHIU, *The Roman, Hindu, and Chinese Law of Adoption* (1930) 10 NAT. U. L. REV. 3, (1931) 11 NAT. U. L. REV. 3. (A comparative study.)

CLAYTON, *Adoption—Relation it Creates—Effect on Property Rights* (1931) 3 MISS. L. J. 238. (Status and inheritance as well as relationship of adopter and child depend on the petition, in Mississippi, though the few cases that have arisen incline to liberality.)

CUTTER, *The Law of Adoption in Massachusetts* (1935) 15 B. U. L. REV. 171. (Editorial discussion of several cases illustrates the theory that both child and community benefit from adoption and emphasizes that regulations should preserve the dual advantage.)

DESENBERG, *Procedure of Adoption and Rights of Adopted Child* (1932) 7 NOTRE DAME LAWY. 223. (A brief article touching such points as methods of adoption, rights as to support and inheritance, status.)

EPSTEIN, *Rights of Adopted Children under "Lapsed Legacy" Statutes* (1936) 25 CALIF. L. REV. 81. (A theoretical discussion involving definition of terms.)

EVANS, *Testamentary Revocation by Adoption of Child* (1934) 22 KY. L. J. 600. (Points out the need of considering both adoption and testamentary revocation statutes.)

GOODRICH, *Legitimation and Adoption in the Conflict of Laws* (1924) 22 MICH. L. REV. 637. (Shows how decisions concerning legitimation are frequently cited and relied upon in questions of adoption, particularly those that involve domicile and inheritance.)

HARRINGTON, *Rights of Adopted Children in Illinois to Federal Old-Age Benefits* (1938) 3 JOHN MARSHALL L. Q. 491. (Looks at Illinois adoption laws regarding inheritance.)

HUBERT, *Rights of Descendants of Adopted Children in Louisiana in the Estate of the Adoptive Parent* (1934) 8 TULANE L. REV. 431. (Reviews the history of adoption in Louisiana by way of answering the question whether adoption creates a descending line beyond the first degree.)

HUTTON, *Concerning Adoption and Adopted Persons as Heirs in Pennsylvania* (1937) 42 DICK. L. REV. 12. (An important Supreme Court decision provokes discussion of the right of adopted persons to inherit from collateral adoptive kindred. The case caused a departure from beaten paths of inheritance law in giving more rights to the adoptee.)

LIMBAUGH, *Adoption of Children in Missouri* (1937) 2 MO. L. REV. 300. (A résumé of adoption practices in Missouri, 1857–1937.)

LONG, *Adoption as Affecting Inheritance in Pennsylvania* (1935) 39 DICK. L. REV. 179. (A discussion of inheritance rights of adopted persons in Pennsylvania in the light of court decisions as well as of the statutes.)

LYMAN, *Conflicts of Law and Facts with Special Application to Adoption Statutes* (1935) 9 CONN. B. J. 315. (Looks at the effect of revised probate laws which give the adopted child the same rights of inheritance as a natural child.)

McFARLANE, *The Mississippi Law on Adoptions* (1938) 10 MISS. L. J. 239. (The article contrasts the Mississippi law of adoption with laws of other states and suggests improvements.)

NEVAS, *Adopted Children Unprovided for in Wills* (1936) 21 CORNELL L. Q. 346. (Limited to rights of after-born children not mentioned in wills and to saving legacies under lapsed statutes, showing a trend toward after-born, or in some states, after-adopted children sharing with the adoptee.)

NEWBOLD, *Jurisdictional and Social Aspects of Adoption* (1927) 11 MINN. L. REV. 605. (Calls attention to some of the gaps in legal and judicial machinery of adoption with the conclusion that adoption laws are inadequate and improperly interpreted, perhaps because they lack such sponsoring as pressure groups give to their interests.)

O'GRADY and BERRY, *Adoption Proceedings in the District of Columbia* (1937) 26 GEO. L. J. 119. (Compares the 1937 Code with older adoption legislation in D. C., against a background of the new versus the old in many states.)

SNIDER, *Abrogation of Adoption* (1936) 16 B. U. L. REV. 700. (An editorial points out that while adoption procedure and abrogation are regulated by law yet the problem is a social one. Permanence is implied in the parent-child relationship, of which adoption is an imitation.)

LEGIS. *Legislation and Decisions on Inheritance Rights of Adopted Children* (1936) 22 IOWA L. REV. 145. (Looks at some of the main inheritance problems of the adopted person, traces principles and tendencies, suggests a three-point statute.)

CASE NOTES AND COMMENT

(1926) 5 N. C. L. REV. 67. (Involves inheritance by natural parents from an adopted child whose property derived from his adoptive parents.)

(1926) 12 VA. L. REV. 511. (Some of the involvements of laws of descent and distribution in an adoptive family are indicated.)

(1927) 21 ILL. L. REV. 525. (Courts in several states have enforced adoption by contract, to protect the adopted child, even though final legal steps have never been taken.)

(1928) 6 CAN. B. REV. 166. (Concerns the validity of an adoption agreement entered into prior to the existence of an adoption statute.)

(1928) 6 CAN. B. REV. 729. (Indicates international complexities arising over property willed in Saskatchewan, where no adoption statute existed, to a child adopted under the laws of the state of Washington.)

(1930) 43 HARV. L. REV. 652. (Emphasizes the need of strict compliance with the statutes by pointing out that an adopted person may fail to inherit because of the cumulative effect of several weaknesses in the details of his adoption, no one of which would necessarily disqualify him.)

(1931) 15 MINN. L. REV. 719. (Questions the right of natural parents to see their child after his adoption when the interests of the child and the validity of the contract conflict.)

(1931) 6 WASH. L. REV. 94. (Discusses inheritance by the adopted child both "from" and "through" his adoptive parents.)

(1932) 20 CALIF. L. REV. 327. (Argues against inheritance by the adopted child from his adoptive relatives.)

(1932) 18 VA. L. REV. 677. (Compares states which cling to the idea of consanguinity in descent with those that allow inheritance from collateral adoptive relatives.)

(1933) 18 MINN. L. REV. 67. (Inheritance from an adopted child by the adoptive versus the natural family.)

(1933) 3 IDAHO L. REV. 264. (Failure of an adopted child to qualify as an heir because the adoption had never been completed according to statute.)

(1934) 2 DUKE B. ASSN. J. 17. (Indicates that inheritance by the adopted child is precarious unless statutory requirements have been met, or inheritance has been specified.)

(1936) 10 TEMPLE L. Q. 311. (Brings out the uncertainty of inheritance by adopted children even when the statute seems clearly to indicate such right.)

(1936) 14 N. Y. U. L. Q. REV. 117. (Involves the question of whether the words "child" or "descendant" are limited to mean blood relations or may include adopted children, in a will.)

(1937) 11 TEMPLE L. Q. 572. (Discusses a leading case which broadens the rights of the adopted child and overrules the common law "call of the blood" as sole determinant of inheritance rights.)

(1937) 50 HARV. L. REV. 1200. (Inheritance and adoption between the states.)

(1938) 16 CHICAGO-KENT REV. 198. (Contrasts conflicting Supreme Court decisions in Illinois and New York.)

(1938) 36 MICH. L. REV. 1408. (Case notes regarding the right of natural parents to see their child after his adoption.)

(1938) 10 ROCKY MT. L. REV. 208 (Notes on a case concerning the right of an adopted daughter to insurance from the estate of her adoptive father point out controlling provisions as to inheritance.)

General Index

Index of Names

www.ingramcontent.com/pod-product-compliance
Lightning Source LLC
Chambersburg PA
CBHW021814270326
41932CB00007B/186